D0115828

GALATIANS

Joyce Meyer's Biblical Study Series

Ephesians
James
Galatians
Colossians

GALATIANS

A Biblical Study

BY JOYCE MEYER

Faith
Words

NEW YORK NASHVILLE

Copyright © 2020 by Joyce Meyer

Cover copyright © 2020 by Hachette Book Group, Inc.

Hachette Book Group supports the right to free expression and the value of copyright. The purpose of copyright is to encourage writers and artists to produce the creative works that enrich our culture.

The scanning, uploading, and distribution of this book without permission is a theft of the author's intellectual property. If you would like permission to use material from the book (other than for review purposes), please contact permissions@hbgusa.com. Thank you for your support of the author's rights.

FaithWords
Hachette Book Group
1290 Avenue of the Americas, New York, NY 10104

faithwords.com

twitter.com/faithwords

First Edition: March 2020

FaithWords is a division of Hachette Book Group, Inc. The FaithWords name and logo are trademarks of Hachette Book Group, Inc.

The publisher is not responsible for websites (or their content) that are not owned by the publisher.

The Hachette Speakers Bureau provides a wide range of authors for speaking events. To find out more, go to www.hachettespeakersbureau.com or call (866) 376-6591.

Unless otherwise noted, Scripture quotations are taken from the Holy Bible, New International Version®, NIV®. Copyright ©1973, 1978, 1984, 2011 by Biblica, Inc.™ Used by permission of Zondervan. All rights reserved worldwide. www.zondervan.com The "NIV" and "New International Version" are trademarks registered in the United States Patent and Trademark Office by Biblica, Inc.™

Scripture quotations marked AMP are taken from the Amplified Bible. Copyright 2015 by The Lockman Foundation. Used by permission.

Scripture quotations marked AMPC are taken from the Amplified® Bible, Classic Edition. Copyright © 1954, 1958, 1962, 1964, 1965, 1987 by The Lockman Foundation. Used by permission. www.Lockman.org

Scripture quotations marked NKJV are taken from the New King James Version®. Copyright © 1982 by Thomas Nelson. Used by permission. All rights reserved.

Library of Congress Cataloging-in-Publication Data has been applied for.

ISBNs: 978-1-5460-2608-2 (hardcover), 978-1-5460-2607-5 (ebook)

Printed in the United States of America

LSC-C

10 9 8 7 6 5 4 3 2 1

CONTENTS

ABOUT GALATIANS

Author: *Paul*
Date: *AD 53–57*
Audience: *Christians in the province of Galatia*

The books of Romans and Galatians are closely linked in content, and both were written by the apostle Paul. In Romans, Paul opens to us the fullness of the gospel of grace, and in Galatians, he defends that gospel because it has come under attack by people seeking to draw the early Christian believers back into legalism. Paul probably wrote both letters from Corinth while he was ministering there.

We can see that Paul was passionate about ministering the gospel as much as he possibly could. While he was in one place teaching, he was thinking about and ministering to churches in other cities through writing letters to them. Paul worked hard toward his goal of seeing people saved by grace through faith and presenting everyone "fully mature in Christ" (Col. 1:28–29), and he frequently mentions how often he prayed for the believers in every city.

Paul emphasizes in both Romans and Galatians that not only are we justified by faith, but we must learn to live by faith as well. I like to say that we should not reserve our faith only for times of trouble when we need God's help, nor merely for our initial salvation, but we should learn over time as the Holy Spirit teaches us to do everything we do by faith. We are to continually abide in Christ and rely on Him to help us at all times and in all things. Paul even goes so far as to say that whatever is not of faith is sin (Rom. 14:23).

Paul had been to Galatia two times and hoped to go again, but the Holy Spirit sent him elsewhere. When he first went to Galatia, the people there were idol worshippers, but by God's grace Paul was able to bring many of them to a saving knowledge of the Lord Jesus Christ through preaching. We can see from this example that when people are led by the Holy Spirit, they don't always get to do what they want to do or what they think is best, but they submit to the Spirit's leading. Paul tried on several occasions to go to certain places to preach the gospel, but he said that the Holy Spirit prevented him and sent him somewhere he had not planned to go (Acts 16:6–10). Freedom to follow the Holy Spirit in our daily lives is exactly what Paul is trying to remind the Galatians that they are free to do, and in order to be free we must not submit to legalism—a set of rules and regulations about how everything involving our relationship with God must be done.

Under the Old Covenant, the Israelites lived under the law. It seems there was a rule about almost everything they had to do, and they were proud of their ability to keep the rules.

However, the problem was that no one could keep them *all*. Therefore no one could ever be justified before God through the law. But Paul announced that God had provided a solution: He sent His Son to pay for the sin of mankind, and by grace though faith in Jesus, the perfect Son of God, salvation is available to all who will believe in Him and put their trust in Him.

Salvation is a free gift, but many people found that truth difficult to believe. Even if they accepted Christ, they tried to add some of the old laws to their faith, so in essence their so-called faith became no faith at all. We live by one or by the other—faith or the law—but mixing the two does not work. Paul says in Galatians that he died to the law in order to live to Christ (Gal. 2:19). When Jesus died on the cross He said, "It is finished" (John 19:30), meaning He had fulfilled the law, and now God's children could be free from the ceremonial rules and regulations they had once been required to perform.

Sometimes when people enthusiastically receive Christ, they go through times of severe testing shortly afterward. This was the case with the Galatians, as certain men began telling them they had to submit to the Law of Moses and that they must be circumcised, as the Jews had been, in order to have a covenant relationship with God. The Jews believed and taught that Gentiles had to become Jewish before they could become Christians. In short, their gospel was Jesus plus the Law of Moses. The truth is, we need Jesus only, not Jesus plus something else, in order to be saved.

Satan always comes and attempts to steal our faith in a variety of ways. That is certainly easier for him to do with new believers who haven't had time to become rooted and grounded in their faith. But Paul encourages people throughout his writings to stand firm in the truth they have learned and not to fall back into the bondage from which they have been delivered.

The Book of Galatians has had a profound effect on many people, including some prominent Christians we read about and learn from. Martin Luther, the father of the Reformation, was one, and another was John Bunyan, the famous Puritan preacher and author of *The Pilgrim's Progress*. Many scholars consider Galatians to be "the Magna Carta of Christian Liberty," according to sermoncentral.com.

It is always good to read the Bible, but studying it is much better. We need to dig deeper into the Book of Galatians, as well as the rest of the Bible, and when we do we will find hidden treasures that not only help us live for God better but also continually make us more and more free to enjoy God and the life He has provided for us through Jesus.

Jesus came to give us a new way to live, one filled with life and power, with righteousness, peace, and joy. This is the way of faith in Christ by which we receive complete forgiveness for our sins and assurance of eternal life. In this new way, we have the freedom and privilege of being led and guided by the Holy Spirit rather than following written rules and regulations.

Jesus sacrificed Himself on the Cross and died there,

bearing the burden and punishment of our sins. As promised, He rose from the dead on the third day and is now seated at the right hand of God. On Pentecost, another promise was fulfilled and our Heavenly Father sent the Holy Spirit to be in us and with us at all times (Acts 2:1–33)—to teach us, help us, comfort us, and guide and lead us in all things. This was good news for the Galatians, but some of the Jews were having a hard time accepting the new life in Christ and continued hanging on to their old legalistic ways, trying to convince those who were following Christ that they were wrong.

In this book I will discuss the problem with works of the flesh, which occur when we use our own human energy to try to accomplish what only God can do. Martin Luther, whom God used to bring about the Protestant Reformation, was a man who experienced the agony of trying to work his way into right standing with God by doing every conceivable thing he could think of (works of the flesh) and finding that none of it gave him a clean conscience or assurance of God's acceptance. He was miserable and tormented until he discovered the gospel of grace and realized that Christianity is not about what we can do for God, but what He has done for us.

People who seek acceptance from God through their own works live by fleshly efforts that leave them exhausted, worn-out, and frustrated. I like to call works of the flesh "works that don't work."

In Galatians, Paul also deals with many practical issues of everyday life. He addresses topics such as the danger of people-pleasing, reaping what we sow, the proper way to deal with people's faults, avoiding self-righteous attitudes, compromise, love, walking in the Spirit, and many others.

I believe you will find the Book of Galatians very helpful in your personal walk with God, and my prayer is that it will help you in your journey toward being formed into the image of Jesus Christ and being His personal representative during your time on earth. I also believe you will learn to enjoy your walk with God and the life He has provided through Jesus.

This book is meant to be studied, and you will find various Scripture references throughout the manuscript that will deepen your understanding of what that particular section of the book is teaching if you choose to take time to look them up.

Key Truths in Galatians

- Our relationship with God is based on grace, not law. We are to reject legalism and embrace grace in every area of our lives.
- In Christ, we can be set free and we can stay free.
- We are to walk in the Spirit, not in the flesh.
- We reap what we sow.

CHAPTER 1

CALLED BY GOD

Qualified by God

Galatians 1:1–2

*Paul, an apostle—sent not from men nor by a man, but
by Jesus Christ and God the Father, who raised him from
the dead—and all the brothers and sisters with me, to the
churches in Galatia:*

Paul begins this letter to the Galatians as he does some of his
other epistles, by establishing in the first sentence that he is
an apostle called by God, not by man. I am sure he does this
because there were many who questioned his commission
and authority. Where did he get the right to teach others,
especially since he had formerly persecuted the church of
Jesus Christ? What qualified him?

Many are called into the gospel ministry in much the same
way as Paul. God calls them and qualifies them by anointing them for a special task. This perplexes those who don't
understand that God chooses who He uses for reasons that
often make no sense to us. Paul's past as one who persecuted
Christians certainly did not qualify him. It actually would
have disqualified him had that been the criteria for God being
able to use him.

Having a sinful past prior to receiving Jesus as Savior and
Lord does not disqualify anyone from being used by God.

In fact, it may actually help us have compassion for those who are deceived and are living sinful lives, as we once were, and who need to be rescued and restored. Nothing helps us understand someone in trouble more than having had the same trouble ourselves.

Paul teaches that God chooses and uses what the world considers foolish in order to show the folly of worldly wisdom (1 Cor. 1:27–28). Those whom God chooses to use for His work are very different from those the world would choose. God often chooses people who do not have the right qualifications for the job based on worldly standards, but they do have the right heart. Their motives are pure, and they love Jesus greatly.

When God was ready to replace King Saul, He told the prophet Samuel that He would anoint someone from the house of Jesse as the new king (1 Sam. 16:1). Samuel went and examined all of Jesse's sons one by one. God rejected each one, so he asked if any of the brothers were not there. The one God chose was the one the family believed was so unlikely they had not even brought him in from the field for consideration. The one God chose was named David, and Samuel anointed him to be king (1 Sam. 16:1–13). God doesn't look on the outward man, but on the heart (v. 7), and David had a heart filled with desire for God.

We might say Paul also had a heart for God, and he had formerly been a zealous and committed Pharisee. He had a lot of zeal for God, but it was zeal without knowledge. Although he had done many terrible things, he actually believed he was serving God as he did them. When Jesus confronted him on the Damascus road, he was quick to repent and ready to do whatever Jesus asked him to do (Acts 9:1–19). After this encounter with the living Christ, Paul was never the same. He was saved by grace, certainly not by any of his own good works. He was deeply convinced of the truth that we are saved by grace alone and not by our works, and his mission in life became to teach others that same truth.

No one is more qualified to teach others a truth than those who have firsthand experience with what they are trying to teach. Paul had a fire in him that no amount of criticism or judgment from others could put out. He was called by God— not by man—to teach the message of grace; therefore, man could not stop what God had begun.

If you have been invited to do a job for God, you can be assured that nothing in your past can hinder you. God sees your heart, and He sees who you are becoming, not merely who you have been in the past. If we wish to walk with God, we must look forward. We have no eyes in the back of our head, and we might let that convince us that we are not to spend our lives looking back but, rather, looking to the future. Don't look at the wrong things you have done; look at the right things you can do.

Personal Reflection

In what ways are you qualified for God to use you? How could He use your past to help others?

_____

_____

_____

_____

_____

_____

_____

Grace and Peace

Galatians 1:3–5

*Grace and peace to you from God our Father and the Lord
Jesus Christ, who gave himself for our sins to rescue us
from the present evil age, according to the will of our God
and Father, to whom be glory forever and ever. Amen.*

Paul adds his normal and frequent greeting, "Grace and
peace to you from God our Father and the Lord Jesus Christ."
His greeting was much more beneficial to its recipients than
most of our greetings might be today. We may greet a person
with the words *hello* or *hi*, but Paul wishes those he meets the
power of amazing grace in their lives and the peace of God,
which is truly wonderful.

Unless we understand grace, we will never have peace,
and Paul desires peace for every person. After all, what is
life really worth if we don't have peace? No matter what else
we have—power, position, riches, influential friends, or
possessions—it is worth nothing if we don't have peace to
go along with it. Peace leads us to joy, and I think what every
person desires above all else is to be happy. Paul says that
the Kingdom of God is not about meat and drink (things),
but righteousness, peace, and joy in the Holy Spirit (Rom.
14:17), and to that I say, "Amen!" We want to know that we

are right with God and to have peace and joy. As Matthew 6:33 teaches us, if we will seek first the Kingdom of God and His way of being and doing, all the other things we desire will be added to us. The psalmist says, "Delight yourself also in the LORD, and He shall give you the desires of your heart" (Ps. 37:4 NKJV).

Sadly, we often spend a great deal of our lives searching for what we think will make us happy, but we find once we obtain each thing, it is unable to provide us with what we thought it would. We go from possession to possession, job to job, relationship to relationship, or even religion to religion searching and searching, but all the while the simplicity of the gospel is available if we will open our eyes and see it. God created us for His pleasure and ours, and nothing else will ever satisfy us except a deep and intimate relationship with Him, putting Him and His will first in all things. This world is not our home, and I doubt that we can ever be completely satisfied as long as we dwell here. In fact, as believers in Christ, I think a part of us is always longing for our eternal home where we will see Jesus face-to-face.

Consider this Scripture verse and then ask yourself if you are pursuing the right things in your life:

Do not love the world or anything in the world. If anyone loves the world, love for the Father is not in them. For everything in the world—the lust of the flesh, the lust of the eyes, and the pride of life—comes not from the Father but from the world. The world and its desires

pass away, but whoever does the will of God lives
forever.

1 John 2:15–17

I urge everyone to spend their time on earth preparing for
eternity. If we spend our time merely trying to have what the
world offers, we will always end up disappointed. We may
and should enjoy the things of the world, but God must
always come first. I like to say, "Enjoy whatever God gives
you as much as possible, but don't become so attached to it
that you feel you cannot be happy without it."

I remember quite often that everything I purchase is
already in the process of decay and that it is not eternal. If
you ever wonder if that is true, just drive by a junkyard and
consider that all the junk you are looking at was once someone's dream. It was shiny and new, but now it is old, worn-
out, and forgotten. Let us remember what Jesus says: "Do not
store up for yourselves treasures on earth, where moths and
vermin destroy, and where thieves break in and steal. But
store up for yourselves treasures in heaven, where moths and
vermin do not destroy, and where thieves do not break in
and steal" (Matt. 6:19–20).

In his greeting to the Galatians, Paul says that Jesus gave
Himself so that we might be delivered from this present evil
world according to the will of God (Gal. 1:4). Although we
sojourn here for a period of time, we are to be in the world
but not of it (John 17:14–16). You might say that those of us
who are saved by God's grace remain here to help the world,

not to expect the world to help us. We can bring joy to the world by sharing the good news of the gospel, but the world cannot bring true lasting joy to us. The important thing is to not get attached to it and to always remember that we are merely passing through. Before long we will all stand before God. What an amazingly wonderful day that will be! Then and only then can we be completely satisfied. Through Christ we can be content while we are on earth, but our complete satisfaction is only found in Him.

Personal Reflection

In what ways are you seeking God above all else?

_____

_____

_____

_____

_____

_____

_____

CHAPTER 2

◆—◇—◆

NO OTHER GOSPEL

No Other Gospel

Galatians 1:6–9

*I am astonished that you are so quickly deserting the
one who called you to live in the grace of Christ and are
turning to a different gospel—which is really no gospel at
all. Evidently some people are throwing you into confusion
and are trying to pervert the gospel of Christ. But even if
we or an angel from heaven should preach a gospel other
than the one we preached to you, let them be under God's
curse! As we have already said, so now I say again: If
anybody is preaching to you a gospel other than what you
accepted, let them be under God's curse!*

Paul uses strong words in attempting to convey to the Galatians the danger of accepting or even entertaining the idea
that any gospel other than the one he has preached to them
has any validity at all. Two times he pronounces a curse on
anyone who preaches another gospel. Some might feel that
his strong language is in opposition to his message of grace,
but it isn't. Paul knows the danger of deception and does not
want the Galatians to lose their newfound freedom.

We must be firm in what we believe, and although we
should not be narrow-minded and unwilling to learn new

things, neither can we be so open-minded that we are ready to believe anything we hear or read.

Paul isn't actually cursing people, but by divine inspiration of the Holy Spirit he is pronouncing that divine judgment must fall on anyone who leads others into error. The pure unadulterated message of the gospel of Jesus Christ is the only true gospel, and anything that teaches that we need Jesus plus something else will lead us in the wrong direction. Of course, we should obey God and pray and other such things, but those spiritual activities do not save us. We are saved by God's grace through faith in Jesus Christ (Eph. 2:8–9).

Paul begins this section with "I am astonished." Philip Graham Ryken in the *Reformed Expository Commentary: Galatians* says Paul is what the English would call gobsmacked. *Gob* is slang for mouth and to be *smacked* is to be slapped with an open hand. So someone who is gobsmacked, opens his mouth, puts his hand over it, and lifts his eyebrows in amazement. Paul was gobsmacked. His astonishment regarding how quickly the Galatians were entertaining anything other than what he had taught them was very concerning to him. He couldn't be with them all the time, and he wanted them to be strong enough in their faith that they would not believe lies tempting them to believe any other doctrine.

The Jews who held the belief that it was good to have Jesus as long as certain Jewish laws were also followed were called Judaizers, and Paul considered them dangerous to anyone who was not firmly and deeply rooted in the truth regarding salvation. One reason Paul was so astonished was that his missionary trip to Galatia had been one of his most successful. Sinners were saved, miracles were performed, and churches were planted. He could hardly believe that after what the Galatians had witnessed and experienced, they could so quickly begin falling away.

Paul was angry, and that is understandable. No one wants to see their hard work turned to ashes, and he wanted to communicate with the Galatians as soon as possible to wake them up. I have heard it said that the church's greatest troublemakers (both now and then) are not those outside the church who criticize, oppose, ridicule, and persecute it, but those inside who try to change or pervert the gospel—people who take sound theology and twist or distort it. They don't totally deny it, but they add to it or take away just enough to turn it into a false doctrine without the people even realizing what is going on.

Excessive reasoning can cause a person to start believing false doctrines. Faith is a matter of the heart, not the head. For example, I've never seen God, but I know He is real. I did not see Jesus die on the cross, but I know He did. I know that God is good, even though there are bad things that happen in this world. I know God loves me and that He always will. How do I know these things? God's Word tells me they are true, and I know in my heart they are true. Faith believes what it does not see in the natural realm; it is "the substance of things hoped for, the evidence of things not seen" (Heb. 11:1 NKJV).

The Galatians had experienced the freedom Jesus gave to them and they knew His peace and joy, so why would they return to the bondage of following religious laws, rules, and regulations? The Jews who had crept in among them made a persuasive argument, and they started thinking too much instead of continuing in simple faith.

You may or may not be familiar with the term *the law*. I want to make sure you understand what I am talking about when I use it and give a few examples you might relate to. Paul is talking about the ceremonial laws of the Old Covenant—laws the Jews had with God. He wanted those he taught to know they had been set free from the law through Jesus. However, not everyone believed that, and they were busy trying to force people to believe they still had to follow those same laws.

The Jews had to follow many rules and regulations in order to be acceptable to God. In addition to these laws, we are capable of making laws of our own and trying to force them on other people, as well as following them ourselves. When we make a law out of anything, we always feel guilty if we don't follow the rule we have established. For instance, some churches believe it is wrong for a woman to cut her hair or wear makeup, jewelry, or even colorful and attractive clothes. Any woman attending those churches must follow those rules or she is made to believe she is unacceptable to God. Paul writes in 1 Corinthians 11:4–5 that it is wrong for a man to pray with his head covered and wrong for a woman to pray with her head uncovered. The reason for this is that doing so would have made women equal with men, and in the culture Paul was addressing, it would have been inappropriate; a woman's hair was not to be cut short or shaved (1 Cor. 11:5–6). Thankfully, we know that Jesus has set women free, and there is no longer male or female because we are all equal in Christ (Gal. 3:28). But in Paul's day, the culture had not yet changed, and he did not wish to cause problems over certain customs because he had something much more important to teach the believers.

Paul was also the one who said a woman should not adorn herself by braiding her hair or wearing expensive gold, pearls, or apparel, but that she should adorn herself modestly and be more concerned with having beauty on the inside rather than outside (1 Tim. 2:9; see also 1 Pet. 3:3–4). Once again, this was a cultural issue, because in those days most of the women who had elaborate hairstyles and wore lots of jewelry and expensive clothing were prostitutes. Paul wanted the women of God to dress in a manner that would leave no room for judgment.

Our culture is different now, and guidelines about appearances don't apply to us in the same way they did to people in Paul's day. Of course, people today should dress appropriately and not in a manner that would cause others to lust after them or that would bring undue attention to them. God created lots of colors, and surely He meant for them to be enjoyed. Our clothes do not need to be drab and colorless; they simply need to be appropriate.

I had an aunt who believed certain things were wrong,

such as wearing colored eye shadow, so she always corrected me when she saw me wearing it. She and my uncle did not drink any alcohol, but they also refused to even go into a restaurant that had a bar in it and felt that eating in those restaurants was wrong for others also. They watched television at home but refused to go inside a movie theater. These types of practices are personal preferences and should not be forced on other people or used to make them feel guilty. The things we should all avoid are the things mentioned in Scripture, not things other Christians decide on their own should be avoided. I know some people who fast one day every week, but they don't tell other people they need to do the same. God may ask us to do or not do certain things that are personal to us, and we should keep them between the Lord and ourselves and simply be obedient to Him without imposing those personal convictions on others.

We can make a law out of anything, and when we do, we always feel guilty if we don't keep it. We also tend to judge harshly others who don't do as we do, and Paul teaches that we have no right to do that (Rom. 14:4). He writes that all things are permissible, "but not all things are beneficial *or* advantageous...constructive [to character] *and* edifying [to spiritual life]" (1 Cor. 10:23 AMP). In Paul's day, some people thought eating meat was sinful, and others felt they were free to eat meat, so Paul said let everyone be "fully convinced in his own mind" (Rom. 14:5) and that we should not judge one another over these matters (Rom. 14:13). If you want to read more about these issues, you will find broader explanation in Romans 14, 1 Corinthians 8, and 1 Corinthians 10:20–31.

God Is Not for Sale

If we let our flesh have its way, rather than walking by the Spirit, it will always look for some way to get at least some of the credit for doing good deeds and being a good person. When we are proud of the works of our flesh, we usually judge others who are not doing things the way we do them. We should humbly receive the goodness of God knowing that we don't deserve it, and we should respond to His goodness by doing all we can for God because we love Him and because of all He has done for us, not for any other reason.

Because human nature is flawed and wants to earn or deserve what we get, convincing people that they need to do one thing or another to be saved and acceptable to God is easy, and the devil takes advantage of that weakness if we let him. There are, of course, good things we do, but we do them because of what God has done for us by His grace, not in order to get something from Him. God is not for sale, and we cannot buy His favor with any amount of good works—it's a gift. And God's favor—His love, grace, and mercy toward us—is not a gift if it has a price tag.

Pride that drives us to try to earn God's love and forgiveness is dangerous because it can keep us from experiencing true freedom in Christ to become everything we are created to be. Think of it like this: If you give someone wrong directions to a location they want to get to, they will get lost. If that can happen in terms of physical locations, just imagine what can happen to us spiritually if we are given wrong directions about receiving new life in Christ and follow them without question.

I heard a story about a woman who was very anxious that she and her child would miss their train stop. She asked the conductor if he would make sure she got off at the right place, and he said he would. Another man sitting nearby told her that he would help her because the workers on the train often had so much to do they might forget her. At a certain stop, the man told her it was the place she needed to get off the train, and he helped her with her child and their luggage.

The train continued and came to another stop, and the conductor came back to look for the woman. He was surprised by her absence and asked the people around where she was and if they had seen her. The man who had helped her off the train said that since the conductor had not come at the last stop, he had helped her off. The conductor said, "Man, you have made a huge mistake! That was not a regular stop, it was an emergency stop we made for another purpose, and you have left the woman at a very dangerous place where she may be attacked by wild animals."

This story helps us understand what can happen to us if we listen to the wrong people. The apostle John encourages us not to believe every spirit, but to test them to make sure they represent the truth of the gospel (1 John 4:1).

It is sad to say, but too many people who start off right

concerning their belief about salvation through Jesus end up deceived. They have been miserable in their lives of sin and self-effort and have had the gospel preached to them, believed it, repented of their sin, and received Christ as Savior and Lord. They go along happily for a while and begin to grow in knowledge concerning Christ and the new way of living He offers. The devil hates this, so he puts someone in their midst who presents another message that includes their current beliefs, but adds something to it that, if believed, will cause them to get lost as the woman on the train did.

I have found that a simple check of my motives as to why I am doing certain things helps me stay on the right track. Am I doing what I do to get something from God or to give something to Him? Paul tells the Corinthians that any work done with a wrong motive will be burned up in the fire on Judgment Day and there will be no reward for it (1 Cor. 3:13). I don't want to waste my time doing things and then losing my reward; I would rather face the truth about why I am doing what I do and make sure I am not doing it as a law I feel I must keep out of some false religious obligation.

I want to encourage you to receive the gift of God's love, grace, and mercy and follow the leading of the Holy Spirit in every area of your life. Make a determined decision to steadfastly put your trust in what Jesus has done for you and not in works of the flesh that can never make you right with God. That's the only way you can have the life of righteousness, peace, and joy in the Spirit of God that Jesus died to give you!

CHAPTER 3

PAUL'S CONVERSION

Live to Please God

Galatians 1:10

Am I now trying to win the approval of human beings,
or of God? Or am I trying to please people? If I were still
trying to please people, I would not be a servant of Christ.

Paul is firm in declaring that in his ministry, he does not seek to please people, but to please God. He actually says that if he were trying to be popular with people, he would not have become an apostle. This makes me wonder how many people miss their true calling from God because they choose to please people instead of Him.

When God called me to teach His Word, my extended family and friends were not pleased. The church I attended was not pleased, and many people tried to change my mind by making it clear that if I chose to move forward with a ministry of teaching God's Word, I would no longer be welcome in their midst. I was asked to leave my church because God had called me to do something for Him that did not fit into their traditional theology. At the time it hurt me deeply, but later I realized that God used their rejection to get me to a place where I could learn what He wanted me to learn and go on to become the person He wanted me to be.

Paul knew that if he sought people's approval, he might not

get it because of his reputation as a man who hunted Christians in order to arrest and persecute them. Paul was now a changed man, just as many believers are today, but people don't always believe we have changed. Instead they see us as we have been in the past and refuse to see us as new creations in Christ (2 Cor. 5:17). People see what we have been and what we are, but God sees who and what we will become.

The account of Paul's conversion is in Acts 9:1–19, and I think it is important to include it in this section so we can see how completely he was changed by an encounter with the living Christ. I am choosing to tell you his story in my own words, but I also recommend that you read it for yourself.

Paul (known as Saul at this point in his life) was still making threats of persecution and murder against the disciples of the Lord. He had been in attendance at the stoning of Stephen, who was an esteemed disciple in the church. He was glad to see Stephen stoned and perhaps threw some stones himself. He had gotten permission from the high priest of the local synagogue to capture and bring people he found to be believers in Christ to Jerusalem for trial.

As he traveled and approached Damascus, suddenly a light shone from heaven all around him. "He fell to the ground and heard a voice say to him, 'Saul, Saul, why do you persecute me?'" (Acts 9:4). Saul asked who was talking to him, and the Lord said, "I am Jesus, whom you are persecuting... Now get up and go into the city, and you will be told what you must do" (Acts 9:5–6).

Those traveling with Saul were astounded because they

saw no one, yet they heard the voice of Jesus and witnessed what happened to Saul. When he rose from the ground, Saul was blind although his eyes were open. So they led him by the hand into the city of Damascus. For three days, he could see nothing and he did not eat or drink anything.

Now, the Lord had spoken to a disciple named Ananias in Damascus and told him where to find Saul and what to do. Ananias was afraid because he had heard of Saul's violent reputation, but the Lord assured him that He had chosen Saul as His instrument, so Ananias left to find Saul. He went into the house where Saul was and did what God had instructed him to do. He laid his hands on Saul and told him he had been sent by Jesus to lay hands on him so he might regain his sight and be filled with the Holy Spirit. Immediately, something like scales fell from Saul's eyes, and he regained his sight, arose, and was baptized. For some days after that, he remained with the disciples at Damascus and began immediately to proclaim the gospel he had previously persecuted. He declared Jesus to be the Son of God, and all who heard him were amazed.

What a transformation! I would imagine that many of us wish our experience had been so astounding, but God knows what each of us needs and He provides it. I am sure Saul needed something quite spectacular to change his mind, and God met him where he was and gave him what he needed.

Wait on God's Timing

You would think Saul would have headed straight to Jerusalem since that was the center of Christianity, but he didn't.

He was wise enough not to go immediately to present himself to the other apostles. We don't know all the reasons he waited except that he obviously believed it was what the Lord wanted him to do. Faith in Christ was being preached, and the church was growing, but Paul was called to preach with a special emphasis on the grace of God, and I am sure he wanted to make sure it was received well. Timing is always important, and Paul was sensitive to making sure the time was right. This could have been one reason for delaying his travel to Jerusalem, but I think more than anything else he needed time alone with God, allowing Him to speak to him, rather than hearing from other people right away.

Paul also had much to learn, and we see in Galatians 1:17 that he went to Arabia and then returned to Damascus and remained there for three years. We are not given much information about what he did during that time, but I feel sure that our Lord was teaching him a great deal. After the three-year period in Damascus, he did go to Jerusalem because it was revealed to him that he should go. For fifteen days there, he met with Peter, but not with any of the other apostles. Paul and Peter agreed that salvation could be received through faith in Christ, but Paul was a lot more outspoken about the fact that there was no need for circumcision or for the observance of any of the ceremonial laws of Moses.

Although circumcision is not a problem for us today as it was in the early church, some groups of Christians still teach that we must do certain things in addition to what Jesus did in order to be saved. As I mentioned in the previous chapter, we should obey Christ because we love Him and not try to earn or "buy" His love with our good works. He loved us before the foundation of the world, so how could we possibly do anything to deserve what is already ours as a free gift?

I know someone who admits they don't learn anything at the church they attend, and when I asked why they don't go somewhere else, they told me they just could not give up the rituals that they routinely follow in each service they attend. I think it is sad when rituals are more important to us than growing in Christ. For generations the Jews depended on rituals, ceremonies, following rules, and the observance of certain days and feasts to put them in good standing with God. But Paul was trying to get people to realize that the old system (Old Covenant) has been fulfilled through Christ's death and resurrection, and He has provided a new way to have relationship with God through faith in Him apart from observance of the law.

We can see that Paul is using wisdom and obviously being patient and led by the Spirit concerning the timing of when to present himself to more of the church leaders. Waiting on God's timing is challenging for most of us, but Paul did that, and I admire him for it. Paul did not seem to have a need for other people's approval or acceptance of him, and we should all strive for that. If we can listen to God without allowing the approval or disapproval of people to affect us, it is very good. Paul doesn't tell us what he and Peter discussed, but I would imagine it was enlightening to both of them. Paul didn't go to Jerusalem seeking approval, but he did want to be sure that his preaching wouldn't be opposed and perhaps cause confusion. We might say that when he met with Peter he was "testing the waters," so to speak.

Personal Reflection

How are you patiently waiting on God's timing in your life?

_____

_____

_____

_____

_____

_____

_____

Paul Defends His Message

Galatians 1:11–24

*I want you to know, brothers and sisters, that the gospel
I preached is not of human origin. I did not receive it
from any man, nor was I taught it; rather, I received it by
revelation from Jesus Christ. For you have heard of my
previous way of life in Judaism, how intensely I persecuted
the church of God and tried to destroy it. I was advancing
in Judaism beyond many of my own age among my people,
and was extremely zealous for the traditions of my fathers.
But when God, who had set me apart from my mother's
womb and called me by his grace, was pleased to reveal his
Son in me so that I might preach him among the Gentiles,
my immediate response was not to consult any human
being. I did not go up to Jerusalem to see those who were
apostles before I was, but I went into Arabia. Later I
returned to Damascus. Then after three years, I went up to
Jerusalem to get acquainted with Cephas and stayed with
him fifteen days. I saw none of the other apostles—only
James, the Lord's brother. I assure you before God that
what I am writing to you is no lie. Then I went to Syria and
Cilicia. I was personally unknown to the churches of Judea
that are in Christ. They only heard the report: "The man
who formerly persecuted us is now preaching the faith he
once tried to destroy." And they praised God because of me.*

In this section of Galatians Paul describes his defense of his apostleship to the Galatians. For people who are called by God, the need to defend themselves to others is sad, but it happens frequently. Paul never tries to hide who he has been or what he has done in the past. In fact, he feels his past makes his testimony regarding his redemption even more powerful. He readily admits persecuting the church out of zeal for God, but he says that when it pleased God to reveal His Son to him, he was changed forever.

We should never feel the need to hide our past sins, because they are in fact what make our salvation by grace so amazing. Perhaps Paul's past was one reason God chose him as the one through whom to introduce the gospel of grace. There was no better candidate than someone who fully knew he did not—and never could—deserve the goodness that God had shown him. I know from personal experience that when God dramatically changes people, it usually has a profound effect on them, and they seem to be more successful at convincing others of the validity of the gospel message.

Before closing this chapter, I think it would be beneficial to discuss further the wisdom Paul uses concerning how and when to present himself to the other apostles. Too often in our enthusiasm over our salvation, we try too soon to convince others of how much we have changed. We would be wiser to simply live our new beliefs patiently and let others witness for themselves the changes in us.

I know for certain that I was too zealous in the beginning of my newfound life in Christ, and I made comments to friends and family that they did not understand, nor should I have expected them to. This caused division that took years to mend, and we forfeited relationships we could have enjoyed had we handled ourselves with more wisdom. We had plenty of enthusiasm, but we needed more wisdom.

My husband has a friend who is too aggressive in sharing the gospel with people he has only known for a few minutes, and it ends up causing confusion and resistance to him rather than accomplishing his desire to witness to them. He is excited, but in trying to share his enthusiasm with people who have no idea what he is talking about, he does more harm than good.

It is usually best to make sure the timing of our sharing is right. I believe we should be bold in our witness, but we are more likely to be received favorably when we allow the Holy Spirit to guide us and let us know when the timing is right. Without patience, we usually choose our own timing and don't get good results. This is true not only in our witnessing but in many other areas of life as well. The writer of Ecclesiastes tells us there is a perfect time for everything and that everything is beautiful in its time (Eccles. 3:1–11). Paul did present himself to all the apostles at a much later date, and as we will see, when he did the timing was perfect.

CHAPTER 4

FIGHTING FOR FREEDOM

Wilderness University

Galatians 2:1

Then after fourteen years, I went up again to Jerusalem,
this time with Barnabas. I took Titus along also.

In Galatians 2, Paul goes away again, this time for fourteen years. Barnabas and Titus were with him, and I am sure he was ministering to people as he traveled, but he still stayed away from Jerusalem, which at that time was the center of Christianity, until the Holy Spirit once again revealed to him that he should go.

During these years that he was away, God prepared Paul to be confident and bold in his faith in Christ so he could preach the gospel even when he faced great opposition. For example, in Galatians 2:6, Paul says, "As for those who were held in high esteem—whatever they were makes no difference to me; God does not show favoritism—they added nothing to my message." He respected them (namely the original apostles), but did not believe them to be higher or better than he was simply because they had walked with Jesus during His earthly ministry. He knew that what God had done in his life was different from what He had done in Peter's, but it made no difference in how God could and would use each of them to spread the gospel. Paul made no fuss over anyone's credentials because he knew that God shows no partiality.

Paul's Absence

Let's think for a few minutes about the purpose of Paul's three-year absence and then his fourteen years away from Jerusalem. I call it Wilderness University. It seems that most of the people God uses mightily are hidden from the world for a season. Some refer to this period of time as "the silent years." People who go through such an experience have a vision of what they are supposed to do, but God will not release them yet to do it. He usually puts them in a less-than-desirable place and uses it to teach them and train them for the ministry He has prepared for them. During these times it's easy to think we are in the wrong place because it's not a place of comfort for us, but more often than not we are exactly where God wants us. When God prepares something for us, then He has to prepare us for it!

David was anointed to be king twenty years before he wore the crown, and most of those years were spent hiding from King Saul, who was jealous of him and continually sought an opportunity to kill him (1 Sam. 16–27:12).

Joseph had a dream from God and was sold into slavery by his own brothers, who were jealous of him, but God had him right where He wanted him. Joseph experienced approximately thirteen wilderness years before he graduated to the position God had been preparing him for, and many of those years were spent in prison for a crime he did not commit (Gen. 37–41).

Moses was in the wilderness for forty years before he was allowed to lead the Israelites out of Egypt, where they had been in slavery for many long and painful years (Ex. 2:11–3:10; Acts 7:29–34).

John the Baptist was in the wilderness for many years before his public ministry started. Even Jesus was hidden from the world for most of the thirty years before His public ministry began, and then it only lasted about three years (Mark 1:2–6). But those years were so powerful they are still having a profound effect today and will always continue to do so.

When I say people are often hidden, that doesn't mean they are totally alone, but that they are not known by large numbers of people and are not doing great things as far as the world can see. But doing a small thing faithfully and in secret is a great thing to God. During these so-called hidden years, people are being prepared for the future, and we all need that time of preparation. If you have a dream in your heart and feel invisible, as though no one knows you or cares who you are, don't despair. Let God use this time to teach you and draw you closer to Him. While you are waiting, do anything He asks you to do without concern about how small it is or who knows you are doing it. As long as God knows, that is all that really matters.

In today's society, talented people are often put on platforms and admired by the masses long before they are mature enough to properly handle the visibility and acclaim. Sadly, this is frequently the cause of their ultimate failure. People tend to be very impatient and have a sense of entitlement rather than being willing to spend the years it may take to be prepared for the promotion God desires to give them when they are ready.

Personal Reflection

Explain what you have learned during the wilderness seasons you have been through.

_____

_____

_____

_____

_____

_____

Paul, the Freedom Fighter

Galatians 2:2–9

I went in response to a revelation and, meeting privately with those esteemed as leaders, I presented to them the gospel that I preach among the Gentiles. I wanted to be sure I was not running and had not been running my race in vain. Yet not even Titus, who was with me, was compelled to be circumcised, even though he was a Greek. This matter arose because some false believers had infiltrated our ranks to spy on the freedom we have in Christ Jesus and to make us slaves. We did not give in to them for a moment, so that the truth of the gospel might be preserved for you. As for those who were held in high esteem—whatever they were makes no difference to me; God does not show favoritism— they added nothing to my message. On the contrary, they recognized that I had been entrusted with the task of preaching the gospel to the uncircumcised, just as Peter had been to the circumcised. For God, who was at work in Peter as an apostle to the circumcised, was also at work in me as an apostle to the Gentiles. James, Cephas and John, those esteemed as pillars, gave me and Barnabas the right hand of fellowship when they recognized the grace given to me. They agreed that we should go to the Gentiles, and they to the circumcised.

Paul was sent to the Gentiles (the uncircumcised), just as Peter was sent to the Jewish people (the circumcised). Both of their calls were equally important, but very different in administration. In the same way, we must realize that we are all responsible to do only what God gives us to do, not to compete with others or try to do what they are doing.

Many of the Jews were adamant that the Gentiles had to be circumcised even though Jesus died to free them from the law and from Old Testament rituals (Gal. 3:13–14). Paul stands firm for freedom from the law, from rules and regulations, and insists that people are now free to follow the guidance of the Holy Spirit. He emphasizes that salvation is by grace alone and that nothing needs to be added or even could be added to what Jesus did on the Cross. Paul's purpose is to reveal that the Gentiles are to be included in the plan of salvation, and it is difficult for us to understand how unbelievable and shocking this was to the Jews of his day.

The Jews and Gentiles had hated one another throughout history, and the Jews considered the Gentiles no better than dogs. But their attitude had to change because in Christ, there is no more Jew or Greek, male or female, slave or free, but we are all one in Him (Gal. 3:28). Our worth and value are found in Christ, and in nothing else—not in our ethnic background, our talent, who we know, our level of education, our gender, or anything else, but Christ alone.

The Galatians received salvation through Paul's message, but some of the Jews were trying to bring them into bondage under the law. They wanted them to be circumcised, but Paul fought for their freedom. Because the devil wants us in bondage to religious rules and regulations, we must fight for our freedom. He frequently makes suggestions to us regarding other things we might be required to do—like praying for a specified amount of time daily or reading a certain number of chapters in the Bible each day. Although these things are good and beneficial, they don't get us to heaven. They are not required for salvation.

When we receive Jesus and the Holy Spirit comes to fill our hearts, we get a new "want to." We *want* to do the right thing, we *want* to study God's Word and talk with Him in prayer, and we *want* to help other people. Just think about it for a moment. When we read and study the Bible, we are not doing it for God; we're doing it for ourselves so we can grow spiritually and gain knowledge of God's will. When we pray, we don't do that for God; we do it to help ourselves and others and for the simple pleasure of spending time with Him. Prayer is a privilege, not an obligation.

Jesus says He came to set captives free (Luke 4:18). This freedom is not the freedom to do whatever we like whenever we want to, but it does mean we are free to follow the guidance of the Holy Spirit. That kind of life is exciting and filled with power, but following rules, making sacrifices, mutilating the flesh, and other such disciplines as the Old Covenant required will always leave us disappointed because no one can become right with God through them. No matter how many rules we keep, there is always one we miss, and God's Word states that if are guilty of breaking one rule or part of the law, then we are guilty of breaking them all (James 2:10).

When we do something because we feel it is what God wants us to do, we can do it with joy. Philippians 4:13 promises that Jesus will always give us the strength to do anything He asks us to do. But if we do something because we feel that God will be angry with us if we don't, then our motivation is entirely wrong.

In *The Message of Galatians*, John Stott wrote, "The Christian has been set free from the law in the sense that his acceptance before God depends entirely upon God's grace in the death of Jesus Christ received by faith. To introduce the works of the law and make our acceptance depend on our obedience to rules and regulations was to bring a free man into bondage again."

Don't Forget the Poor
Galatians 2:10

All they asked was that we should continue to remember
the poor, the very thing I had been eager to do all along.

After Paul met with the other apostles, they perceived that God had given him grace and offered to him the "right hand of fellowship." In other words, they accepted him and his ministry. They all agreed that Paul would go to the Gentiles and the others would go to the Jews. They had only one request, which was for Paul not to forget the poor. He was already helping the poor and was eager to continue.

Why would they mention helping the poor as the one thing they wanted to be sure Paul didn't forget? I have learned over the years that those who are poor have a special place in God's heart, just as orphans and widows and anyone who is hurting does. Just think about it. If you had five children, wouldn't your heart be drawn toward the one who was hurting the most? You would love all your children the same, but if one of them was hurting, you'd hurt with him or her. Your thoughts would be focused on that one, and at times you may even feel a physical aching in your soul when you thought about his or her pain.

God mandates us to help the poor and says that if we do,

He considers what we do for them as if we've done it unto Him (Matt. 25:40). So, if we truly want to serve God, we must be ready to help people who need it. One way I believe we can show our gratitude to God for all He has done for us is by helping those who are less fortunate than we are. No matter how many problems you have, you probably know someone who is worse off than you are. Reaching out to them not only helps and encourages them; it helps you also. God's Word teaches us that it is more blessed to give than to receive (Acts 20:35). If we believe that, then giving should be a normal part of our lifestyle.

Personal Reflection

What can you do to help or give to people in need around you?

_____

_____

_____

_____

_____

_____

CHAPTER 5

—◦—

JUSTIFICATION BY FAITH

The Danger of Being a Compromiser

Galatians 2:11–14

When Cephas came to Antioch, I opposed him to his face, because he stood condemned. For before certain men came from James, he used to eat with the Gentiles. But when they arrived, he began to draw back and separate himself from the Gentiles because he was afraid of those who belonged to the circumcision group. The other Jews joined him in his hypocrisy, so that by their hypocrisy even Barnabas was led astray. When I saw that they were not acting in line with the truth of the gospel, I said to Cephas in front of them all, "You are a Jew, yet you live like a Gentile and not like a Jew. How is it, then, that you force Gentiles to follow Jewish customs?"

Paul "opposed" Cephas (Peter) in Antioch because Peter behaved one way with the Gentiles and another with the Jews (Gal. 2:11–12). This passage tells us that when Peter ate with the Gentiles, he did not follow Jewish food regulations. But when Jewish Christians came from James, Peter separated himself from the Gentiles for fear of what the Jewish believers might do, thinking they might reject him or judge him critically—and he didn't want that. We know from other instances in Peter's life that he struggled with fear of what people thought of him.

Paul, on the other hand, seemed to not care what people thought of him as long as he knew in his heart that he was following God's will. Paul was loving, but he was also swift to speak the truth, and he did not approve of anyone being two-faced.

Leaders have influence over the people who admire them, and many of the Jews acted hypocritically when they observed Peter's influence. The hypocrisy must have been rampant because it affected even Barnabas, and he was led astray. Not only did Paul confront Peter, but he confronted him in front of the others. I don't think his intent was to embarrass Peter, but to let everyone know that the kind of behavior Peter exhibited was not acceptable. Paul was definitely a strong leader who said what he meant and meant what he said, and anyone who wishes to follow Jesus must be the same way, because this is the example Jesus gave us also (John 2:13–17). Sincerity, not pretense, is what God requires.

People can give many reasons that seem logical for the things they say and do, but if their behavior is not in line with God's Word, it is wrong. Peter and the others may have said, "We don't want to offend the Jews," or, "We want to show them love," but no excuse for hypocrisy is acceptable to God. Hypocrisy is something unbelievers in every era have accused Christians of, and it causes many people to be resistant to Christianity. It is vitally important that we live our lives in front of people according to what we say we believe and not compromise to gain their approval. Some unbelievers will tempt you to compromise and then disrespect you for doing so. I urge you to resist the temptation to compromise in order to gain the approval of any person or group of people. Be a God-pleaser, not a people-pleaser.

Personal Reflection

Do you struggle with people-pleasing, or do you live to please God? Explain why or why not.

_____

_____

_____

_____

_____

_____

Faith Alone

Galatians 2:15–19

We who are Jews by birth and not sinful Gentiles know that a person is not justified by the works of the law, but by faith in Jesus Christ. So we, too, have put our faith in Christ Jesus that we may be justified by faith in Christ and not by the works of the law, because by the works of the law no one will be justified. But if, in seeking to be justified in Christ, we Jews find ourselves also among the sinners, doesn't that mean that Christ promotes sin? Absolutely not! If I rebuild what I destroyed, then I really would be a lawbreaker. For through the law I died to the law so that I might live for God.

Paul emphatically reminds us that—whether Jew or Gentile—we are justified by faith alone and not by works of the law. I have been deeply impacted by Paul's statement that we must die to the law in order to live to Christ (Gal. 2:19–20). We cannot mix law and grace and ever enjoy the kind of life Jesus died to give us. For years, I was a staunch rule keeper and somewhat legalistic in my ways. But when I realized I had to die to following the law if I wanted to be free to fully follow Christ, it helped me to see how important it is.

For example, for a long time I tried to pray for one hour

and read six chapters of the Bible each day. I felt proud when I succeeded and guilty when I failed. That is what happens when we view spiritual activities as laws instead of privileges. I don't watch the clock anymore. I simply pray and read until I feel full and satisfied in my spirit. This is similar to how I feel when I have had enough to eat at a meal. God's Word and time with Him is our spiritual food. I don't count how many minutes I eat dinner, and I don't count how many minutes I pray or study the Bible.

One of the most difficult concepts for most of us to grasp is that we are saved by grace through faith and not by any kind of work we do (Eph. 2:8–9). We have been taught all of our lives that we must work hard and earn what we get. In so-called normal life in the world, that principle is correct, but in spiritual life it is not. God does want us to work, and we will receive rewards for the work we do on earth, but those works do not save us. To be justified means to be just as though we have never sinned. God sees us through Christ if we believe in Him. In other words, He sees us made right with Him and justified through Christ. This truth is so marvelous that it takes most of us a number of years to fully believe it. That's why we keep trying to earn what is already ours by the grace of God instead of simply receiving it by faith.

To help me understand this, the Lord once told me I was trying to get into a chair I was already sitting in. That word picture helped me grasp what I was doing. I spent many miserable years as a believer who was serving God in ministry, feeling guilty because I failed to always keep rules that made me feel like a good Christian, rules I had actually made for myself. Often, even if we believe we are free from the ceremonial Law of Moses, we make up our own laws and impose them on ourselves and on others as well.

The law came written on stone tablets. Like the stone they were originally written on, laws are harsh and impossible to keep perfectly. But Jesus fulfilled the law for us and has written God's law on our hearts. He has made us sensitive to His touch. Ezekiel 36:26–27 says, "I will give you a new heart and put a new spirit in you; I will remove from you your heart of stone and give you a heart of flesh. And I will put my Spirit in you and move you to follow my decrees and be careful to keep my laws." The laws God speaks of here are moral rules (guidelines), and His Spirit, the Holy Spirit who now lives in the children of God, makes us aware of God's will and helps us fulfill it.

Anyone who is born again through faith in Christ instinctively knows right from wrong in most instances. We do grow and learn more and more all the time, but the Holy Spirit who lives in us will guide us if we will pay close attention to Him.

Dying to Live

Galatians 2:20

I have been crucified with Christ and I no longer live, but Christ lives in me. The life I now live in the body, I live by faith in the Son of God, who loved me and gave himself for me.

Paul says he has been crucified with Christ and that he no longer lives, but Christ lives in him; the life Paul now lives in the body he lives "by faith in the Son of God" (Gal. 2:20). In essence Paul is saying that he wants God's will more than he wants his own will and that he is willing to die to anything that is not God's will for him. When we die to ourselves, we cease having relationship with anything. So dying to self means that we cease having relationship with what we want if it doesn't agree with what God wants.

Some people feel this takes away their freedom, but it actually sets us free. Whatever God wants for us will always be best in the end, even if we cannot see it in the beginning. *Real life in Christ* is much more than merely walking around and breathing. God wants us to have and enjoy an amazing life filled with His righteousness, peace, joy, good fruit, success, and a close, intimate relationship with Him.

Dying to live is simply saying no to self and yes to God. Paul calls it "dying" because it is painful. We feel things in our flesh, and even when we give up something that is hurting us, it may still be painful for us to give it up. For example, you might have a certain group of friends who are actually holding you back from a deeper walk with God. If He leads you away from them, it may hurt even though you know it is right. Learning to trust men was hard for me because I was abused by my father and I had a rebellious attitude, which was hard for me to give up. But holding on to that attitude would have kept me out of God's will, and anytime we are out of God's will we will be miserable. Learning this helps us to surrender our will to His will.

The healing of our wounded souls comes in degrees of glory as we learn to let go of wrong behavior and attitudes and be obedient to God (2 Cor. 3:17–18).

Personal Reflection

How will you say no to self and yes to God?

_____

_____

_____

_____

_____

Don't Frustrate God's Grace

Galatians 2:21

*I do not set aside the grace of God, for if righteousness
could be gained through the law, Christ died for nothing!*

Paul ends this section of his letter to the Galatians with an
interesting comment. He does not frustrate and "set aside the
grace of God." If we continue to think we need to add our
works to Christ's sacrifice, then we are not receiving God's
amazing grace and, therefore, making it of no value. Paul says
he will not do that, but he will receive the grace of God in every
area of his life and live by faith. Considering all the suffering
Jesus endured in order to make His grace available to us, for
us to not receive it would be a tragedy.

More and more grace is available to us. All we need to do
is admit that we are helpless without Jesus and receive His
grace, not only to save us but to enable us to do whatever
we need to do in life. Grace is not only "the riches of God at
Christ's expense" or the favor of God, but it is also power to
perform God's will.

You may remember that when Paul writes to the Corinthians about his thorn in the flesh, he tells them that he
begged God three times to remove it (2 Cor. 12:7–8). Then
Paul quickly adds that God said, "My grace (My favor and

loving-kindness and mercy) is enough for you [sufficient against any danger and enables you to bear the trouble manfully]" (2 Cor. 12:9 AMPC).

Do you want to bear your troubles with more maturity? Do you want to stop feeling guilty each time you make a mistake? Do you want to love your life? Do you want to stop frustrating the grace of God? If so, then realize that you are saved by God's grace alone through faith and that this is the way you must learn to live.

CHAPTER 6

HOW CAN I CHANGE?

The Key to Real Change

Galatians 3:1–4

You foolish Galatians! Who has bewitched you? Before your very eyes Jesus Christ was clearly portrayed as crucified. I would like to learn just one thing from you: Did you receive the Spirit by the works of the law, or by believing what you heard? Are you so foolish? After beginning by means of the Spirit, are you now trying to finish by means of the flesh? Have you experienced so much in vain—if it really was in vain?

I want to begin by saying that Galatians 3:1–9, which I first learned in the Amplified Bible Classic Edition, was life-transforming for me. I learned through these verses that I could never change myself through struggle, self-effort, discipline, or anything else without God's help. He had begun a good work in me, and He would finish it (Phil. 1:6). I don't mean that we don't make an effort to change when needed or that we don't discipline ourselves, because we will need to do that, but we cannot do it without Jesus. We need His grace (help) in order to change. Change doesn't come by our trying to change; it comes as we learn our new identity in Christ and allow the Holy Spirit to work out of us what God has placed in us.

We may receive salvation by grace alone but then try to perfect ourselves through our own efforts. We should want to change and be more like Jesus; I would doubt the salvation of anyone who did not desire that. But no one can do God's job for Him.

Paul writes to the Philippians, telling them to "continue to work out your salvation with fear and trembling," not in their own strength, "for it is God who works in you to will and to act in order to fulfill his good purpose" (Phil. 2:12–13).

As one little boy said, "You can't work out what hasn't been worked in." His statement is brilliant and especially true in our relationship with God. He would never expect us to behave righteously unless He had given us righteousness. He would not expect us to show forth the fruit of the Holy Spirit if He hadn't given us the Holy Spirit. He fills our hearts with His love and then asks us to love others. We cannot give away what we don't have, so God works in us and we work with the Holy Spirit to work out what is in us. Once the good things God has given us by His grace are worked all the way through us, then other people can see Jesus through us, and they become thirsty for what they see. Jesus says we are to be salt and light (Matt. 5:13–16). Salt is designed to make people thirsty, in addition to adding flavor to food. Are you flavoring your home, the place where you work, your school, or neighborhood? Are you making others thirsty for Jesus by letting Him live through you?

What does Paul mean when he writes that we are to work out our salvation with "fear and trembling"? The Amplified

Bible Classic Edition version of Philippians 2:12 brings great clarification, and I want you to read it and think about what it says.

> ...Work out (cultivate, carry out to the goal, and fully complete) your own salvation with reverence *and* awe and trembling (self-distrust, with serious caution, tenderness of conscience, watchfulness against temptation, timidly shrinking from whatever might offend God and discredit the name of Christ).

When Jesus ascended to heaven (Mark 16:19; John 14:28; Acts 1:2), He sent the Holy Spirit to live in us (Acts 1:4–5). He is our Teacher (John 14:26). He is the One who convicts us of sin and convinces us of righteousness (John 16:8). He is our Helper and Comforter, our Advocate, and we can do nothing apart from His help (John 14:16–17; 15:5). If we follow Him, we will always end up at the right place. Here's a practical example of what I mean: If you are watching something on television and you feel uncomfortable in your spirit, it is the Holy Spirit letting you know that what you're watching is not good for you. Now you have a choice to make. You can keep watching it because it is interesting to you, or you can follow the guidance of the Holy Spirit, trusting that He will always lead you to the best thing for you. Being able to feel the conviction of the Holy Spirit is a great blessing. Without it we wouldn't realize how we need to change, and the thought of remaining the same is much more frightening than changing.

For many believers, the process of change goes something like this: We hear a sermon or read the Bible, we feel convicted of something we are not doing right, we want to change it, and we begin to try to do so. This may sound right, but it is wrong in every way. Why? It is wrong because we have left Jesus out of the picture. We have not asked for His help and direction. What we need to do is hear the Word and let it convict us of sin or something that needs to change in us, repent, and receive God's forgiveness and ask Him to help us change. We need to continue to pray for change to come and study God's Word in the area in which we need help. Because the Word of God acts as medicine to heal our soul.

Think about it like this: If you have a headache, you don't put a bandage on your head; you take an aspirin or some other form of pain-relieving medicine. If you cut your arm, you don't put an aspirin in it; you get the bandages and cover the wound. You can study God's Word in a similar way. If you have a problem with jealousy, anger, disobedience, or lust, study that subject in the Bible, purchase Christian books that deal with it, and pray as you study. The Holy Spirit will use the Word to change you. God's Word teaches us that as we behold Jesus in Scripture, we are changed into His image from one degree of glory to another (2 Cor. 3:18). The word *glory* basically means the manifestation of all the excellencies of God.

I also recommend just spending time with God in His presence, waiting on Him and relying on Him to change you. We always have a choice to make and a part to play in the process of change, but we cannot do it without God's help. You might ask, "What about discipline? Don't I have to discipline myself?" Yes, we do need discipline, but we cannot be successful even at that without God's help. Learn to let "God, help me" be your most frequently prayed prayer.

Personal Reflection

Have you reached the point where you are no longer trying to change yourself but relying on God's grace to change you? Explain why or why not.

_____

_____

_____

_____

_____

_____

Inheriting by Faith

Galatians 3:5–9

So again I ask, does God give you his Spirit and work miracles among you by the works of the law, or by your believing what you heard? So also Abraham "believed God, and it was credited to him as righteousness." Understand, then, that those who have faith are children of Abraham. Scripture foresaw that God would justify the Gentiles by faith, and announced the gospel in advance to Abraham: "All nations will be blessed through you." So those who rely on faith are blessed along with Abraham, the man of faith.

An inheritor is quite different than a laborer. Parents work hard for their money and then usually leave it to their children as an inheritance. The children get what the parents earned. The same principle operates with Jesus and believers. Everything He has is ours. He paid for our sins, and we are free from them simply by believing that Jesus died for them, took our punishment, and rose from the dead victoriously. We don't have to sacrifice to pay for our sins because Jesus sacrificed Himself, and no other sacrifice is or will ever be needed. Understanding this should make us very thankful, and the writer of Hebrews tells us to offer to God the "sacrifice of praise" (Heb. 13:15). The only sacrifice God wants from us under the New Covenant is praise and thanksgiving, and the more we realize what God has done for us by His grace, the more thankful we will be.

How do we inherit? We inherit by faith ... by having child-like faith that what God promises in His Word is true and that if we wait for it patiently, we will get it. You may not be where you want to be right now concerning spiritual matur-ity, but you can be thankful that you are not where you used to be. You are making progress, even if it is only a tiny bit at a time. Celebrate your victories and progress rather than mourning over your failures.

Paul reminds us that God promised Abraham that He would bless him, and that those who are of faith are sons of Abraham and blessed along with Abraham, the man of faith (Gal. 3:7). Jesus is a descendant of Abraham, and the bless-ings promised to him come to us through Jesus Christ.

The covenant God made with Abraham came 430 years prior to God's giving the law to Moses. Abraham inherited by faith, but Moses and the Israelites worked and struggled to keep the law. God's Word doesn't tell us that we inherit the blessings of Moses, but that we inherit the blessings of Abraham. God only gave the law to prove to people that they could not keep it and that they needed a Savior who was yet to come.

I hope to leave my children and grandchildren a nice inher-itance, and the only thing I want from them is their love and respect and some of their time. I think we can easily see that God wants the same from us. And it's so amazing when we realize that no one has seen or imagined all the good things God has prepared for those who love Him (1 Cor. 2:9).

Abraham believed God, and his faith was counted to him as right standing with God (Gal. 3:6). The same holds true for us.

CHAPTER 7

REDEEMED FROM THE CURSE OF THE LAW

Faith That Leads to Freedom

Galatians 3:10–18

*For all who rely on the works of the law are under a curse,
as it is written: "Cursed is everyone who does not continue
to do everything written in the Book of the Law." Clearly no
one who relies on the law is justified before God, because
"the righteous will live by faith." The law is not based on
faith; on the contrary, it says, "The person who does these
things will live by them." Christ redeemed us from the curse
of the law by becoming a curse for us, for it is written:
"Cursed is everyone who is hung on a pole." He redeemed
us in order that the blessing given to Abraham might come
to the Gentiles through Christ Jesus, so that by faith we
might receive the promise of the Spirit. Brothers and sisters,
let me take an example from everyday life. Just as no one
can set aside or add to a human covenant that has been
duly established, so it is in this case. The promises were
spoken to Abraham and to his seed. Scripture does not say
"and to seeds," meaning many people, but "and to your
seed," meaning one person, who is Christ. What I mean is
this: The law, introduced 430 years later, does not set aside
the covenant previously established by God and thus do
away with the promise. For if the inheritance depends on
the law, then it no longer depends on the promise; but God
in his grace gave it to Abraham through a promise.*

A curse is pronounced on all those who rely on their ability to keep the law for salvation, for if we rely on the law, we must keep all of it, and that has proven over and over to be impossible. The works of the law have nothing to do with faith, but they are, in fact, polar opposites. We are either laborers working for our pay, or we are obedient, loving children who inherit from a loving and benevolent Father. Which one sounds best to you?

The righteous person lives by faith (Hab. 2:4; Heb. 10:38; Rom. 1:17), and without faith it is impossible to please God (Heb. 11:6). You may notice that Paul seems to go over and over the same material in his letter to the Galatians, approaching it from a variety of angles. Is he being redundant? Has he forgotten that he has already written about the same thing earlier in his letter? The answer to both questions is no! Paul goes over and over the same material because the works of the law had been so ingrained in the Jews for such a long time that it was no easy task for them to fully accept this new way of approaching God. Many of them believed in Christ but also enforced certain rules and rituals that had become important to them. Remember that they were also slipping in among the Gentiles with whom Paul was working, trying to convince them that although Jesus was good and it was fine to believe in Him, they also had to add their works to their faith. They were told they needed to be circumcised, observe certain feasts, and do other such things to be totally acceptable to God.

It was good for them to hear the truth Paul taught repeatedly. Hearing the same thing over and over again never hurts us because each time we hear it, our minds are renewed a little more. Eventually they will be completely changed, and we will have life-changing revelation, not just information, and no one will be able to take it from us.

It is written that everyone who hangs on a tree is cursed, and Christ became a curse for us (Gal. 3:13; Deut. 21:23), redeeming us, or purchasing us, from the grip of the devil through the sacrifice of His life and the shedding of His blood. Thank God we no longer have to live under the curse of the law!

Doomed to Disappointment

Anyone who tries to serve God through the works of the flesh (trying to keep the law) is under a curse and doomed to disappointment (Gal. 3:10). When we try very hard to do a thing and always fail, we become frustrated and disappointed. No matter how many rules I tried to keep, I always broke one, felt guilty and condemned, and was miserable until I foolishly thought I had done enough good things to make up for the bad one. The problem was that it was a never-ending cycle of trying to be good, failing, thinking I could pay for my failure by feeling guilty, and then trying to be really good to make up for it, only to repeat the whole process again.

Finally, after we have been caught in this cycle long enough, we find ourselves exhausted. Some people even give up trying to serve God. They stop going to church because they are told weekly about more and more things they must do and must not do, but they are never told how to accomplish them. I love

Paul's letter to the Ephesians because the first three chapters are doctrinal, teaching us who we are in Christ, how much we are loved, and how God sees us, and the last three chapters tell us how to behave in light of who we are. We find a similar format in Galatians. I think it is a tragedy to teach new believers in Christ what they should do and how they need to change without first teaching them who they are in Christ, that they are justified and made right with God by grace through faith, and that He loves them unconditionally. When people are rooted in God's love and acceptance, they *want* to change and easily cooperate with the Holy Spirit.

Personal Reflection

Do you live with an awareness of God's love for you and with the assurance that you are accepted unconditionally? How is Galatians 3:10–18 exposing wrong mind-sets and attitudes that have kept you striving to be right with God through your own effort?

Two Old Preachers

Two old preachers were sitting in a boat discussing whether salvation was of works or of grace. The man rowing the boat listened to them and observed that they were unable to come to a conclusion, so the preachers asked him what he thought. He gave this explanation: I have two oars. I'll call one faith and the other one works. If I pull on the one oar, the boat goes around and around in circles. If I pull on the other one, the boat goes around and around in the other direction but still in a circle; however, if I use them both together, I will get across the river.

This is a good story if you are trying to get across a river, but we are trying to get to heaven, and that is by grace and grace alone. However, I think the story is a good example of how faith without works is dead (James 2:14–23). We need to do good works because otherwise people cannot see our faith. But faith always has to come first, or the supposed good works will turn out to be disappointing, and they will be "works that don't work."

Guarded by the Law

Galatians 3:19–26

Why, then, was the law given at all? It was added because of transgressions until the Seed to whom the promise referred had come. The law was given through angels and entrusted to a mediator. A mediator, however, implies more than one party; but God is one. Is the law, therefore, opposed to the promises of God? Absolutely not! For if a law had been given that could impart life, then righteousness would certainly have come by the law. But Scripture has locked up everything under the control of sin, so that what was promised, being given through faith in Jesus Christ, might be given to those who believe. Before the coming of this faith, we were held in custody under the law, locked up until the faith that was to come would be revealed. So the law was our guardian until Christ came that we might be justified by faith. Now that this faith has come, we are no longer under a guardian. So in Christ Jesus you are all children of God through faith.

The law was useful until grace came. It helped people realize they needed a Savior and a Helper, because they continually failed at keeping every provision of the law. However, Paul says the law was a guardian for us until grace came through

Jesus Christ. You might say that the law helped curtail the riotous nature of sin to some degree, though not entirely.

If people cannot manage their freedom properly, they are actually better off following rules that help keep them in line. This is why it is so important for us to realize that freedom from the law doesn't mean we are free to do whatever we choose to do. We have a new law that guides us, the royal law of love (James 2:8). If we walk in love, we will do no harm to anyone. Paul tells the Galatians that faith works and is energized by love (Gal. 5:6). So faith, if it has no love, is useless. Faith and works absolutely go together, but it is important that we not put the cart before the horse, so to speak.

Discipline is good, and without it we will never become who we want to be. God has given us a spirit of discipline and self-control (2 Tim. 1:7). But we can start out with discipline and end up with rigid rules if we are not careful.

If any law could have made people right with God, we would not need a Savior. The law only guarded us until the fullness of time when God sent His Son to redeem us from the curse of the law.

In addition to religious laws you may have put yourself under, you may have other laws you have made for yourself. For example:

- Do you have to see a certain number on the scale daily or you become upset?
- Do you have to look perfect and have your home in perfect order?

- Do you have to have everything on your to-do list checked off daily?
- Do you have to have all your work done before you think you deserve to rest or take a break?

We impose many standards such as these on ourselves. Having a goal or exercising discipline is good, but it will end badly if it becomes legalism that determines our sense of self-worth.

Equality

Galatians 3:27–29

For all of you who were baptized into Christ have clothed yourselves with Christ. There is neither Jew nor Gentile, neither slave nor free, nor is there male and female, for you are all one in Christ Jesus. If you belong to Christ, then you are Abraham's seed, and heirs according to the promise.

Many people today are fighting for equality, but those who belong to Christ, who are "in Him" through faith, have already been made equal by Jesus. In Christ, we are all one and made complete, and we need not be like anyone else. I admit that people, even those who are born again, don't always treat everyone as equals, but the way people treat us is not what determines our worth. The only thing that truly matters is how God sees us and how we see ourselves. We should never see ourselves as better than others, but neither are we beneath anyone else. We are simply "in Christ."

Our world is filled with division, and that is a shame because it weakens us. We are made stronger as we unite, not as we divide. Satan is the author of division, and we need to work toward unity in order to defeat him. Do you have unity or division within your family? What about in your church or at your workplace? Unity is a pleasant thing, and it is where

God's blessings and His anointing flow (Ps. 133). Be certain that you are never part of the cause of strife and division, but instead stand against it and work for peace.

The three issues that divide people most are race, rank, and gender. The ancient Israelites had a prayer they prayed daily: "Thank God I am not a Gentile, a woman, or a slave." They saw themselves as better than other people, but they were not.

Paul settles the matter and puts an end to class distinction and inequality when he writes, "There is neither Jew nor Gentile, neither slave nor free, nor is there male and female," but we "are all one in Christ Jesus" (Gal. 3:28). It is a mistake to measure ourselves against anyone else. Each of us is a unique individual created in God's image. Real freedom is not found in our circumstances, but in our hearts. Some people confined to a prison cell enjoy more freedom than others living in the outside world because they know their true worth in God's eyes. You are not less than or inferior to anyone else unless you believe you are.

No matter our gender, race, or position in life, we believers in Jesus are all brothers and sisters, and we are part of one another. We should all be careful not to think more highly of ourselves than we ought to (Rom. 12:3) and to never make anyone feel devalued or diminished through our words or behavior.

Let me encourage you to broaden your circle of inclusion and not befriend only those who are just like you are. The wealthy can fellowship with the poor, the young with the old, the highly educated with the uneducated, one race with another, and so on. Treat all people as valuable, because Jesus does.

Personal Reflection

Do you treat everyone as equal and valuable? What are some examples of how you treat people equally?

_____

_____

_____

_____

_____

_____

CHAPTER 8

—◦—

ARE WE SERVANTS
OR SONS?

The Privileges of Maturity
Galatians 4:1–3

*What I am saying is that as long as an heir is underage,
he is no different from a slave, although he owns the whole
estate. The heir is subject to guardians and trustees until
the time set by his father. So also, when we were underage,
we were in slavery under the elemental spiritual forces of
the world.*

In this section of the epistle to the Galatians, Paul makes a
clear and helpful distinction between the Old Covenant and
the New Covenant. Under the old way, people labored while
seeking to serve God and be acceptable to Him through
keeping the Law of Moses. But under the new way, we receive
Jesus by faith and are born again and made new creations.
We become inheritors rather than laborers.

Paul gives us a practical example we can easily understand. If a son is underage, even though he is the inheritor of
an entire estate, he functions as a child, which is not much
different than functioning as a servant. He may in fact be
cared for and expected to live in obedience to the household
servants, who often have more authority than he has because
of his immaturity and youth.

If a father leaves an inheritance to his sons or daughters and those children are underage or very young, then when he dies, the children will find that he has made provision in his will for them but they will be under trustees until they mature. Had the father not made this provision, the children could waste the inheritance and perhaps bring shame on the family name due to their immaturity and young age.

We are much the same in our relationship as sons and daughters of Father God. Jesus, His firstborn Son, has inherited everything the Father has, and we are co-heirs with Him through faith.

> For those who are led by the Spirit of God are the children of God. The Spirit you received does not make you slaves, so that you live in fear again; rather, the Spirit you received brought about your adoption to sonship. And by him we cry, "*Abba*, Father." The Spirit himself testifies with our spirit that we are God's children. Now if we are children, then we are heirs—heirs of God and co-heirs with Christ, if indeed we share in his sufferings in order that we may also share in his glory.
>
> Romans 8:14–17

Spiritual maturity is important, and we mature as we work with the Holy Spirit to lay aside childish ways and learn to be led by God's Holy Spirit into a lifestyle that represents who Christ is and shows the world what He is like.

The Scripture above tells us that we must suffer in order to be glorified. This simply refers to dying to self and using our free will to choose the will of God, no matter how we feel. As we know, children live by their feelings and usually display a great deal of selfishness and disobedience. But, as they mature, they learn to put aside these childish ways and to behave as mature men and women with responsibility.

Under the Old Covenant, people were enslaved to laws, rules, and regulations, but as children born again through faith in Jesus, we are no longer slaves but sons. How do we know we are sons? The Holy Spirit is the Spirit of adoption, and through His work in us, we are aware in our heart that God is our Father (Rom. 8:15–16).

I am fond of a Scripture that says that even if my natural father and mother forsake me, God will take me up and adopt me as His child (Ps. 27:10). Since my parents were abusers and incapable of genuine love, I am very glad to have a heavenly Father who loves me unconditionally and completely accepts me.

Children live under rules to keep them going in the right direction, but as they mature, they learn to follow their father's heart and the rules they have previously lived under are lifted. When my children were young, they each had a list of chores they were expected to do as part of the family. As they matured, they no longer needed the lists because they knew in their hearts what to do.

The purpose of the law was to impress upon people their duties and responsibilities to a holy God, but it had no power to produce a new life in them or to enable them to keep the law. Rather it placed on them an almost intolerable bondage. To be justified by the law that was holy and good in every way, one had to keep it exactly with no deviation. And that was impossible.

Under the Old Covenant, the people were laborers working hard to earn God's acceptance, but under the New Covenant, they received the free gift of righteousness through their faith in Christ. Those who have received Jesus through faith are adopted as sons and daughters, heirs of the Most High God. They have the right to a full inheritance, but the privileges of that inheritance will be released to them little by little as they mature spiritually.

Personal Reflection

Do you have the mind-set of a New Covenant believer? How can you tell?

_____

_____

_____

_____

_____

_____

No Other Sacrifice Needed

Galatians 4:4–7

But when the set time had fully come, God sent his Son,
born of a woman, born under the law, to redeem those
under the law, that we might receive adoption to sonship.
Because you are his sons, God sent the Spirit of his Son
into our hearts, the Spirit who calls out, "Abba, Father."
So you are no longer a slave, but God's child; and since you
are his child, God has made you also an heir.

"When the set time had fully come," God sent His Son, born under the law, to be born of a woman under the law (Gal. 4:4). This woman was a virgin, which shows us that the birth of the Son of God is entirely miraculous. He is both fully God because Father God is His father, and He is fully man because of His human heritage of being born to a woman. Jesus lived under the law and kept it perfectly, so He—as a spotless Lamb—could be slain for our sins. When John the Baptist beheld Jesus, he said, "Look, the Lamb of God, who takes away the sin of the world!" (John 1:29). The Jews understood this because under the Old Covenant, the priest sacrificed a spotless lamb without blemish to God for the sins of the people each year. Under that old system, the ritual had to be repeated over and over, yet it never completely cleansed anyone's conscience. We might say the old system swept sin under the rug. It was always there, even though it was hidden.

Jesus, the Lamb of God who came to take away the sin of the world, did it once and for all, and no other sacrifice is ever needed. So because we are in Christ, we have kept the law perfectly and are now free from it.

We are sons and daughters, no longer slaves to rituals and rules. What good news! Jesus purchased our redemption, and with the Holy Spirit's help, we will mature spiritually and be able to walk in and enjoy all that Jesus died to give us.

It is my great delight to teach people who are believers how to mature so they may enjoy the life Jesus died to give them. I was a miserable Christian for many years because I continued to live by rules and regulations rather than living through and for Christ. But thank God He sets us free! For "if the Son sets you free, you will be free indeed" (John 8:36).

How does this freedom manifest in our lives? Jesus gives us the answer in John 8:31–32. He said that as we continue in His Word, then we are His disciples, and we will know the truth, and the truth will make us free.

God's Word is truth (John 17:17), and as we learn and follow it, we experience greater levels of freedom and joy. Paul writes that when he was a child he behaved in childish ways, but when he became a man, he put aside those childish ways (1 Cor. 13:11).

I believe the most urgent thing for all believers is to focus on spiritual maturity. God didn't save us so we could spend our lives trying to get Him to give us what we want, but in order that we might do His will. He wants us to use our free will to choose His will. Spiritual maturity is not only God's will for us; it is also the only way to truly enjoy our inheritance from God and be light in a dark and desperately needy world.

If God is dealing with you about doing or not doing something, you are aware of it in your heart and conscience. You may try to ignore it, but it is always present, quietly reminding you of your disobedience—and your conscience condemns you. Obeying God isn't as difficult as we make it out to be. Once we know what God wants, we surrender to His will, and our flesh may suffer for a period of time, but soon we rejoice exceedingly because we have the assurance that we are in the will of God.

Personal Reflection

How are you intentionally trying to grow in spiritual maturity?

_____

_____

_____

_____

_____

_____

_____

CHAPTER 9

PAUL'S PLEA TO THE CHURCH

Know God

Galatians 4:8–12

*Formerly, when you did not know God, you were slaves to
those who by nature are not gods. But now that you know
God—or rather are known by God—how is it that you
are turning back to those weak and miserable forces? Do
you wish to be enslaved by them all over again? You are
observing special days and months and seasons and years!
I fear for you, that somehow I have wasted my efforts on
you. I plead with you, brothers and sisters, become like me,
for I became like you. You did me no wrong.*

Paul begins this section of his letter to the Galatians by
reminding them of what their lives were like prior to knowing God and being known by Him. True Christianity is not
about knowing *about* God, but *knowing* God. It is having
an intimate personal relationship with Him through Jesus
Christ and being transformed into His image. To know God
intimately and then turn away from Him to return to a life of
bondage to laws and rules is equivalent to worshipping idols,
in Paul's opinion. He is shocked that the Galatians could
even consider such a thing.

Because I have had a long-term intimate relationship with
Jesus, I often wonder why anyone would even want to get out

of bed in the morning if they do not know Him. It seems to me that my life would be completely devoid of meaning if I did not know God and live my life to serve Him.

To know Him means to know His character, which includes qualities such as His love, goodness, grace, mercy, forgiveness, righteousness, peace, joy, holiness, and many other wonderful attributes. We don't merely know them intellectually, but we experience them. God is with us at all times, always ready to help us, and that should give us great comfort and eliminate fear and worry.

Paul mentions being known by God, and this is as wonderful as knowing God. Don't we all want to be known completely by someone who will accept and love us as we are? Of course we do. God knew us before the foundation of the Earth was created. He saw us in the future and has written down every day of our lives. He knows every thought we think before we think it and every word we will speak out of our mouths before we say it. Our Father not only knows us better than anyone else, He knows us even better than we know ourselves. There is no point in trying to hide anything from Him because He already knows it. With God we don't need to pretend, hide, or even make excuses.

Jesus told His disciples that He chose them; they did not choose Him (John 15:16). This does not mean that we have no free will and are compelled to serve God, but it means that everything starts with God. We cannot come to Him unless He draws us.

The way God chooses us can be likened to a couple going

to an orphanage, seeing a child, feeling love for that child, and then choosing that child to become their adopted son or daughter. Paul is trying every way he can think of to help the Galatians understand what they are contemplating giving up. He fears for them and is concerned that all the labor he has put into them has been wasted. Paul sounds as though he is perplexed and confused about how they could even consider such a thing, and he pleads with them as a mother would plead with a wayward child to return to Jesus and depend on Him alone for salvation.

The Galatians had formerly worshipped pagan gods and goddesses. Some believed in astrology and lived by the signs of the zodiac. Others worshipped Zeus, and some worshipped the mother goddess, Zizimene. None of these were really gods at all. They were made of stone—lifeless and unable to communicate—yet the Gentiles seemed to fabricate a god for everything from bearing children to making crops grow. They were usually afraid of these gods they worshipped, and in some cultures even sacrificed their children to them to appease their anger. When anything went wrong in their circumstances, they assumed they had angered the gods. Just think about how awful this life must have been.

Although the Israelites worshipped God, they did so as though they lived under the law. And although that was very different from worshipping idols, Paul knew that the same demonic influences that worked through these idols were now at work through the Judaizers who had crept among them and were trying to draw them back into bondage to the law.

Paul asked them why they had gone back to observing certain days and festivals, to the "weak and beggarly elements" that had once held them in bondage (Gal. 4:9–10 NKJV). They were following certain days on the calendar ritualistically as a matter of religious obligation, and these things had no power.

Celebrating holidays or special days set aside for worshipping God is not wrong, but depending on them as a means of gaining God's favor or acceptance is entirely wrong.

Personal Reflection

What was your life like before you knew God, and how is it different now that you do know Him?

_____

_____

_____

_____

_____

_____

Paul's Sickness

Galatians 4:13–15

As you know, it was because of an illness that I first
preached the gospel to you, and even though my illness was
a trial to you, you did not treat me with contempt or scorn.
Instead, you welcomed me as if I were an angel of God, as
if I were Christ Jesus himself. Where, then, is your blessing
of me now? I can testify that, if you could have done so, you
would have torn out your eyes and given them to me.

It seems that some kind of sickness caused Paul to remain
in Galatia long enough to share the gospel with the people
there. Perhaps he originally planned on just passing through
or resting there for a night on his missionary journey. Paul
reminds them that although his condition was quite loath-
some and apparently difficult to even look at, they loved
him so much they would have pulled out their own eyes and
given them to him (Gal. 4:13–15).

Although we have no specific information about what
Paul's illness was, it apparently had something to do with
his eyes. Perhaps they were very infected and the infection
was oozing out of them, and it may have had a foul odor. Paul
wonders what happened to the love they once had for him.
Pagans often thought someone with a disfigurement was

under demonic influence, but not so with Paul. They did not reject him; they loved him. Or perhaps it would be better to say they loved the Word of God that he brought to them and the love, acceptance, and freedom it gave them. We usually love those who bring God's Word to us, because it is their hard work that helps change our lives, and it is right that we do.

Paul's Love for the Galatians

Galatians 4:16–20

Have I now become your enemy by telling you the truth? Those people are zealous to win you over, but for no good. What they want is to alienate you from us, so that you may have zeal for them. It is fine to be zealous, provided the purpose is good, and to be so always, not just when I am with you. My dear children, for whom I am again in the pains of childbirth until Christ is formed in you, how I wish I could be with you now and change my tone, because I am perplexed about you!

Unfortunately, this situation deteriorated to the point where the Galatians were turning against Paul. I know the pain he felt must have been deep and intense. He felt as though he was their father and they were his children. Paul writes to them as a wounded lover, wondering how he could have become their enemy by simply telling them the truth. A minister's job is to preach and teach the truth of God's Word, even though not everyone wants to hear it. Truth will convict us of sin and require us to change, so if we are not ready to obey it, the truth makes us uncomfortable.

The Judaizers were jealous of Paul and tried to win the Galatians away from him through flattery (Gal. 4:17–18).

Being able to discern when someone is flattering us merely to get something from us rather than having genuine love for us and offering us sincere encouragement is very important.

Paul encourages the Galatians to follow his example of following Christ. He calls them his "dear children" and once again reminds them that he would be in anguish until Christ is formed in them (Gal. 4:19).

To have a pastor who loves us as much as Paul loved those to whom he ministered to may be rare, but if we do, we have a blessing we should greatly value and appreciate.

Personal Reflection

If you've known a pastor or minister who loves you like Paul loved the Galatians, you have experienced a great blessing! But whether you have or haven't been ministered to like this, how does this kind of love reflect God's love for you?

_____

_____

_____

_____

_____

_____

CHAPTER 10

TWO COVENANTS

Two Covenants

Galatians 4:21–31

Tell me, you who want to be under the law, are you not aware of what the law says? For it is written that Abraham had two sons, one by the slave woman and the other by the free woman. His son by the slave woman was born according to the flesh, but his son by the free woman was born as the result of a divine promise. These things are being taken figuratively: The women represent two covenants. One covenant is from Mount Sinai and bears children who are to be slaves: This is Hagar. Now Hagar stands for Mount Sinai in Arabia and corresponds to the present city of Jerusalem, because she is in slavery with her children. But the Jerusalem that is above is free, and she is our mother. For it is written:

> *"Be glad, barren woman,*
> *you who never bore a child;*
> *shout for joy and cry aloud,*
> *you who were never in labor;*
> *because more are the children of the desolate woman*
> *than of her who has a husband."*

Now you, brothers and sisters, like Isaac, are children of promise. At that time the son born according to the flesh persecuted the son born by the power of the Spirit. It is the

same now. But what does Scripture say? "Get rid of the
slave woman and her son, for the slave woman's son will
never share in the inheritance with the free woman's son."
Therefore, brothers and sisters, we are not children of the
slave woman, but of the free woman.

Paul uses a story from the Old Testament to make a major
point to the Galatians. The Jews called Abraham their father.
Centuries before Paul writes to the Galatians, God had made
a promise to Abraham and his descendants. Since the Jews
were descended from Abraham, they felt all the promises
belonged to them and no other race of people. Abraham
walked with God by faith, not according to the law, because
the law wasn't given until 430 years later.

Abram, who would later be called Abraham, lived in a
city called Haran when God called him to leave his family,
who were idol worshippers, and go to a place He would show
him. God promised to bless him and make him a blessing
(Gen. 12:1–4). Abram did leave, and we are told that he did
not "trouble his mind about where he was to go" (Heb. 11:8
AMPC). He followed God day by day in faith. God searches the
earth looking for those He can work with and work through,
and He found such a man in Abram.

In Genesis 15:1–6, God visits Abram again, telling him
that He would be his shield and that his reward would be
"exceedingly great" (v. 1 NKJV). Abram asked God what He
could possibly give him since he was childless and therefore

had no heir to inherit his blessings when he died. He asked God if he would have to leave all he had to a servant in his house. Then the Word of God came to Abram telling him that he would have a child, his very own son to be his heir, and he believed God!

Naturally speaking, having a child would have been impossible for Abram and his wife, Sarai, because they were long past the age when they could have children. But Abram believed God and that faith was counted to him as righteousness (Gen. 15:6). Abram was made righteous by faith in God's promise, just as we are made righteous by placing our faith in Jesus as our Redeemer. He was not made righteous by following the law but by faith.

Abram asked how he would know this promise would come true, and God made a blood covenant with him, swearing by Himself, since there was no one greater to swear by, that it would come to pass (Gen. 15:8–18; Heb. 6:13–14). After that, God told Abram that he was to keep the covenant by circumcising every male eight days old and older (Gen. 17:10–13). He further said that any male that was not circumcised would be cut off from His people because he had broken God's covenant (Gen. 17:14). We see that God did ask Abram to do something to show his faith, but faith came first, and it was his faith, not circumcision, that made him right with God.

Many things done under the Old Covenant were types and shadows of things that would be fulfilled or happen under the New Covenant. Under the Old Covenant, circumcision was a literal cutting away of the flesh. However, under the New Covenant, the believer is expected to no longer walk according to fleshly ways. We also "cut away" the flesh, not with a knife but with daily decisions to live for Christ rather than self.

Abram and Sarai waited a long time and yet no child had come, so they did what we often do: They hatched their own plan to get what they wanted instead of waiting on God (Gen. 16:1–15). Sarai gave her handmaid, Hagar, to Abram as his secondary wife, thinking she could have a child through Hagar. Hagar did become pregnant, and after that she despised and looked with contempt on her mistress, Sarai. Ishmael was the name of the child born from this union, and his name means "war." Abram and Sarai got what they wanted, but it caused them much grief in the years to come.

God is merciful, and once again when Abram was ninety-nine years old, He appeared to him and told him he would be the father of many nations. He changed his name from Abram to Abraham, meaning "Father of a Multitude," and changed Sarai to Sarah, meaning "Princess" (Gen. 17:1–7, 15). Abraham assumed that God meant this promise would come through Ishmael, but he was wrong. Eventually, when Ishmael was about fourteen years old, the promised child was born to Abraham and Sarah, and he was named Isaac, which means "Laughter" (Gen. 21:1–3).

The works of our flesh (our plans) always cause war and trouble, but waiting for God's promise brings happiness and laughter.

Paul uses this story of Abraham to teach the Galatians that the works of the law (flesh) will cause them misery but walking by faith in the promises of God will bring them joy. He said these two children represented two covenants (Gal. 4:24). Ishmael was born of a slave woman, and Isaac was born of one who was free. Hagar represents bondage, while Sarah represents freedom and joy.

This story gives us a clear picture of what our lives will be like if we follow the law instead of walking by faith. For a while, Ishmael and Isaac grew up together, but eventually God told Abraham to cast out the slave woman and her son because he could not inherit with the son of the free woman. I believe all Christians begin their walk with God with a mixture of faith and works, but as we mature, the works of the law (flesh) must be cast out so we can inherit all that God has for us.

I refer to the works of the law as "works of the flesh" because we struggle in the flesh to keep those laws, and our reward is struggle, frustration, disappointment, and failure. But when we learn to live by faith, we experience righteousness, peace, and joy in the Holy Spirit (Rom. 14:17).

We hope the Galatians heeded Paul's warning and turned away from the deception of trying to mix the law with grace, but we have no definitive proof one way or the other. Some experts believe they did, and others say there is no way to be sure. What I would like to say is that they had a choice to make, just as we do once we are presented with the truth. Paul gave them truth, and only they could decide how they would live their lives from that point forward.

This loving warning from the apostle Paul is intended for us today, just as it was for the Galatians. Gaining freedom is one thing, but maintaining it is quite another. Satan constantly tempts us to come back under the law. We repeatedly find it difficult to believe we cannot earn something from God by our good works, but I want to stress again that our works should be done for God because of what He has done for us in Christ, not in order to get Him to do something for us now. All of His promises come to us by His grace. We are partners with God, and He does give us a part to play in seeing His will come to pass. He gives us things to do, but our motive for doing them is most important. We should always obey gladly, with the motive of giving, not getting.

Jesus said that if we love Him, we will obey Him (John 14:15); He did not say, "If you obey Me, I will love you." Rather, "We love Him because He first loved us" (1 John 4:19 NKJV). God's love is a free gift. It fills us, and then—and only then—can we love Him in return. I recommend that every day you take some time to meditate on God's unconditional love for you. Think about it, read about it, and confess Scripture that tells you about it.

We are to be rooted deep in God's love (Eph. 3:17), and when we are, there is nothing, no one, and no amount of trouble in the world that can separate us from the love of God that is ours through Jesus (Rom. 8:35–39). The more we recognize how much God loves us, the more we will gladly obey Him in all things.

Personal Reflection

What choices will you make today that honor God?

_____

_____

_____

_____

_____

_____

_____

CHAPTER 11

FREEDOM GAINED AND MAINTAINED

Refuse to Go Back to the Old Ways

Galatians 5:1

It is for freedom that Christ has set us free. Stand firm,
then, and do not let yourselves be burdened again by a yoke
of slavery.

In Galatians 5 and 6, we see the practical part of Paul's letter. The Galatians had been living free from the law, and he urges them to maintain the freedom they have previously enjoyed. They have been delivered not only from their sins but also from the rules and regulations of the Old Covenant law. As Gentiles, they have not lived under the law of the Old Covenant, but I am sure that as idol worshippers they were very familiar with the legalistic trappings of any religion without Jesus as its center. They certainly were accustomed to making sacrifices to appease the gods they assumed were angry, especially if anything in their circumstances was not good.

They are finally free through receiving Jesus, but Paul wants them to stay that way. Believers in the one true God can now walk in a place they have not walked in before. They are no longer under the law, yet they have the great privilege of being invited to follow the Holy Spirit rather than doing as they please, according to their own flesh. Only through the power of the Holy Spirit can they live holy, righteous lives and glorify God. Now Paul urges them not to be entangled again in the yoke of slavery they have previously put off.

Think about this principle in terms of what we would say to a drug addict who had been in bondage for many years. His life was miserable because he was constantly afraid of not having the drug he depended on. Now, let's say that God moved in his life and through receiving Christ, that person gained complete freedom from the need for drugs. He was no longer in bondage to drugs. How wonderful the freedom was! But after some time went by, some old friends came by and began luring him back into the lifestyle of bondage from which he had escaped. We would plead with him not to turn back to the old miserable way of living, but to remain free. This, in essence, is what Paul is doing. The Galatians were not drug addicts, but they were in great danger of falling back into the bondage of legalism—being motivated to perform certain actions because of fear of displeasing God if they didn't follow religious rules and make sacrifices for their sins. God doesn't want us to serve Him out of fear of His anger but because of our love and appreciation for all He has done and continues to do for us.

Christ is of no value to us at all if we depend on the law to justify us. In that case, He would have died in vain and we would be fallen from grace. Instead, we have the opportunity to live by faith and to know that we are justified and made right with God through our faith in Christ.

Personal Reflection

Do you believe that your faith in God makes you right with Him? Why or why not?

_____

_____

_____

_____

_____

_____

_____

Righteousness Comes through Faith

Galatians 5:2–6

Mark my words! I, Paul, tell you that if you let yourselves be circumcised, Christ will be of no value to you at all. Again I declare to every man who lets himself be circumcised that he is obligated to obey the whole law. You who are trying to be justified by the law have been alienated from Christ; you have fallen away from grace. For through the Spirit we eagerly await by faith the righteousness for which we hope. For in Christ Jesus neither circumcision nor uncircumcision has any value. The only thing that counts is faith expressing itself through love.

Paul goes on to tell his readers that if they were circumcised, circumcision is now worth nothing to them spiritually. He also says that if they were not circumcised, they are not defective in any way because neither circumcision nor uncircumcision gains anything, but only faith that works through love (Gal. 5:6). Whether a person has been a law keeper or an idolater makes no difference, because "all have sinned and fall short of the glory of God" (Rom. 3:23).

How difficult this must have been for the Jews to hear, since their confidence in their acceptance from God had depended entirely on circumcision and keeping the ceremonial law for many generations. They believed they were better than any other race, and they were proud of their law keeping and self-righteousness. Now, suddenly, all their self-effort was of no value, and it was actually a problem. It held them back from what they wanted, which was right standing with God. We cannot have self-righteousness and the righteousness of God through faith in Jesus at the same time.

The Pain of Change

Even good news is difficult to accept if it overturns a belief we have clung to for most of our lives. Change is very hard on human beings, even change that makes things better. We often want and pray for change, and then it frightens us when it comes.

God not only sets us free from bondage to the law; He sets us free from anything that causes bondage in our lives. He does it little by little as we are willing to let go of the things of the past. For most people who have been believers in Jesus for a long time, the list of things they have been set free from is quite long, but most will also tell you that there is pain in change. I usually say we can pick our pain. We either deal with the pain of change or keep the pain of never changing, and we are the ones who must decide which we want. To me, never changing and remaining exactly the same as I am is more frightening than the fear of change.

What do you want to see changed in your life? Whatever it is, it will require that you let go of the old, even though you may temporarily miss it, so you can take hold of the new and give yourself time to grow accustomed to it.

When I left a position at a church where I had been a pastor on staff for five years to go into the ministry I have now, I was sure I was doing the right thing, yet I missed it terribly. When I attended that church on Sundays, I often left feeling depressed, which was confusing. If I had done the right thing, why did I feel so downcast? I was no longer part of the team and was not included in the staff functions, and when I heard about things they were doing together, I felt left out and sad. Because of the way I felt, on several occasions I came very close to being drawn back into the position I had left, but thankfully, God gave me the courage to continue going forward.

Although I was excited about my new venture and had many dreams and visions for ministry that were finally within reach, I was also lonely and often experienced fear concerning many situations. What if I had been foolish and my step of faith didn't work? What if we didn't have enough money? No one was paying me a salary anymore, and I was totally dependent on God alone as my source. Although He was never late, He was often slower than I would have liked when we needed Him to come through for us.

I was up and down emotionally for well over a year and often felt pulled in two directions, but God was merciful to me and taught me that I was in His perfect will and had made the right decision. The pain and confusion I felt were soul ties to the old job and people. My spirit was thrilled, but my soul (mind, will, and emotions) was still hanging on to what it was accustomed to.

I am certain that the same type of scenario took place in the lives of the Jews and was beginning to take place for the Galatians. On one hand, they loved their new freedom, but on the other, they felt drawn back to the old way of living.

Understanding that getting comfortable with change takes time is a big help to us in navigating change well without falling back into what we have been delivered from. As Paul says, "It is for freedom that Christ has set us free. Stand firm, then, and do not let yourselves be burdened again by a yoke of slavery" (Gal. 5:1).

Personal Reflection

List several things you would like to see changed in your life.

_____

_____

_____

_____

_____

_____

CHAPTER 12

——◇——

FAITH WORKING BY LOVE

Avoiding Hindrances to the Truth

Galatians 5:7–8

You were running a good race. Who cut in on you to keep you from obeying the truth? That kind of persuasion does not come from the one who calls you.

In this section of his letter to the Galatians, Paul teaches that liberty is not permission, nor should it be an excuse to sin. He reminds them that at one time they ran their race well, but their reputation has now been damaged. Their earlier enthusiasm, commitment, and love are not as strong as they once were, and they have been deceived and fallen back into old ways through false teaching.

He wants them to think about their situation, so he asks, "Who cut in on you to keep you from obeying the truth?" He knew the answer but wanted them to realize who and what they needed to be aware of in the future. Sometimes, although life was once really good, we find ourselves in a miserable condition and wonder, "How did I get here?" This is a great question to ask ourselves if we take the time to listen to what God shows us.

Taking time to think about our lives and our actions can save us a lot of trouble in the long run. Not doing so is what

causes so many people to keep making the same bad decisions and mistakes over and over.

What lie caused the Galatians to backslide? The lie that
although they had been justified by faith in Jesus, they also
needed to follow the law in order to be sanctified (made holy).
This is a common malady today. Paul covers this in Galatians
3, but it is worth mentioning again simply because it is such
a temptation for most of us.

We receive salvation by grace through faith and then try to
live holy lives by self-effort or works of the flesh as we try to
follow rules and regulations. The fact is that the law has no
power to sanctify us because we have no ability to keep all of
it, and if we break one law, we are guilty of breaking them all.
Just imagine the frustration of living your life trying so hard
to do the right thing, yet no matter how many right things
you do, there is always something that is not right, and that
one wrong thing nullifies all the rest.

Jesus tells a parable of a rich young man who came to Him
and asked what he must do to inherit eternal life (Mark 10:17–
22). Jesus said to keep the commandments and then went on
to list them. The young man responded that he had kept them
all. Jesus, loving him, replied, "One thing you lack...Go, sell
everything you have and give to the poor, and you will have
treasure in heaven. Then come, follow me" (Mark 10:21).

Several things about this parable stand out to me. The first
is that Jesus loved the young man, so it is safe to assume that
everything He told him was to help him. The second is that
although the young man had done many good things, he still

lacked one thing. We all lack something if we depend on our own good works to justify us and give us entrance into eternal life. Jesus asked him to give away all he had to the poor, but the young man went away sad. This occurred because money meant too much to the young man, and Jesus was trying to get him to realize that. I believe that had the young man obeyed Jesus, he would have received back much more than he gave away. I am certain that multitudes of people go away sad, as the young man did, because they are unwilling to obey God.

Jesus' other disciples witnessed this scene, and Peter's comment was, "We have left everything to follow you!" (Mark 10:28). Jesus' response to them is good news for all of us. He told them, "Truly I tell you . . . no one who has left home or brothers or sisters or mother or father or children or fields for me and the gospel will fail to receive a hundred times as much in this present age: homes, brothers, sisters, mothers, children and fields—along with persecutions—and in the age to come eternal life" (Mark 10:29–30).

We see from this statement that we don't have to wait until we get to heaven to receive a reward. Jesus did tell them they would be persecuted while on this earth, but He also said they would be blessed. This doesn't necessarily mean the young man would end up richer than he was. He might have, if the Lord knew that would be best for him. It simply means that he would have had plenty of all that he needed, with peace and joy and all the other spiritual benefits that come with fully obeying God.

Personal Reflection

How did you get to where you are in your life today?

_____

_____

_____

_____

_____

_____

_____

A Little Leaven

Galatians 5:9–12

"A little yeast works through the whole batch of dough." I am confident in the Lord that you will take no other view. The one who is throwing you into confusion, whoever that may be, will have to pay the penalty. Brothers and sisters, if I am still preaching circumcision, why am I still being persecuted? In that case the offense of the cross has been abolished. As for those agitators, I wish they would go the whole way and emasculate themselves!

Paul reminds the Galatians that "a little yeast works through the whole batch of dough" (Gal. 5:9). They understood this analogy because they baked their own bread and knew how yeast affected an entire lump of dough. Yeast causes the dough to be altered and transformed. It changes it. The yeast Paul was speaking of would do the same for the Galatians in their spiritual lives. It would change their beliefs and alter their faith in a way that would be harmful to them.

In His teaching, Jesus mentions three kinds of yeast, or leaven: the leaven of the Pharisees, the leaven of Herod, and the leaven of the Sadducees. The leaven of the Pharisees was mixing grace with law, the leaven of Herod was political corruption and wickedness, and the leaven of the Sadducees was materialism. Indeed, we do need to beware of all of these.

Paul is hopeful the Galatians will turn around and go in the right direction again. Thank God that He is always willing to give us a chance to repent and recover from past foolishness.

Just as a little yeast affects the whole lump of dough, a little error can turn into a big problem. One of the lies that Satan whispers to us frequently is "A little bit won't hurt." He told Jesus that if He would bow to him and worship him "just once" (Luke 4:7 AMPC), He would be richly rewarded. Jesus immediately reminded him that God's Word says we should worship no one but God and serve Him only (Luke 4:8).

The "just once" lie has been used to deceive many people, causing them to compromise. It is the little leaven that eventually works its way into and adversely affects our entire lives. To compromise means to go a little bit below what we know to be right. *Just a little bit*, we think. *Surely that can't hurt.* But it does. One little bit becomes another little bit and another and another, until what began as a little bit becomes a whole lot, and then it brings destruction.

We need to know what we believe and stick to it, no matter what—to draw a line in the sand and not move the line when it becomes inconvenient. I have been serving God in ministry for more than forty years, and I have seen many false doctrines rise up and influence large numbers of people. They have all disappeared now, and some have left a trail of shattered spiritual lives much like the devastation we see after a hurricane has passed through a town. I am sure more false doctrines will come in the future, and it is urgent that we cling more tightly than ever to the truth of God's Word. Satan's attempts to deceive people are not new, and he will never stop, so we need to become really good at quickly recognizing deceit and resisting it.

Personal Reflection

What is the right way to respond when you are tempted to compromise?

Serve One Another through Love

Galatians 5:13–15

You, my brothers and sisters, were called to be free. But do not use your freedom to indulge the flesh; rather, serve one another humbly in love. For the entire law is fulfilled in keeping this one command: "Love your neighbor as yourself." If you bite and devour each other, watch out or you will be destroyed by each other.

I think it is safe to say that other than the gospel regarding salvation through faith in Christ, learning to walk in love is the most important lesson in God's Word. Jesus says that love is the most important commandment (Mark 12:28–31). Paul writes that love is the greatest thing (1 Cor. 13:13), and he tells Timothy that the purpose of their instruction is love that comes from a pure heart (1 Tim. 1:5).

If I were allowed to teach only three messages for the remainder of my life, the first would be that we are saved by grace through our faith in Jesus, and by it we are justified and made right with God. The second would be the importance of spending regular quality time with God. And the third would be receiving God's love, loving Him in return, and walking in love with other people. Thankfully I don't have to limit my teaching to three subjects, but I share this only to show you how important I believe walking in love is.

After we are saved by grace, if we were to focus on this alone, we would avoid most of our problems. Love does no harm to anyone. People who walk in love cannot be unhappy, because they don't have their minds on themselves but on what they can do for God and others. I have often said that we cannot be both selfish and happy at the same time.

This love we speak of is not a carnal love. It is not a feeling, although it may include feelings. It is the same kind of love God gives to us. It is unconditional, everlasting, and powerful. It is called the "royal law" of liberty (James 2:8) because the person who loves will not break any of the commandments. If we love God as we should, we will happily obey Him, and one of His commands is that we should love one another. As a matter of fact, Jesus says, "A new command I give you: Love one another. As I have loved you, so you must love one another. By this everyone will know that you are my disciples, if you love one another" (John 13:34–35).

Love is something that can be seen and felt. It is displayed in a variety of ways. Love is patient, and it always believes the best. Love helps others, it gives, and it is quick to forgive. This is a very basic list, but just those five qualities of love are plenty to think about and ask God to help us do. I highly recommend that we all major in walking in love. This requires intentionality and saying no to self regularly. Let us remember that Jesus said what we have done to others, we have done to Him, and what we have not done to others, we have not done to Him (Matt. 25:40, 45). That is a thought-provoking statement and one that we should take time to meditate on.

This section of Galatians 5 ends with a warning from Paul that if we bite and devour (fight and argue with) one another, it may consume us. A large percentage of the population is angry or resentful about something, and Christians are certainly not immune to these negative feelings. When I ask people at a conference with several thousand in attendance, I am surprised by how many admit they are angry with someone. Anger devours and consumes us, and it often becomes all we think about. Staying angry with your enemies is like taking poison and hoping it will hurt the person who hurt you. So do yourself a favor and forgive. Just as God has forgiven us, so we must forgive others (Eph. 4:32).

Personal Reflection

List some examples of how you may serve others through love.

_____

_____

_____

_____

_____

_____

CHAPTER 13

—◦—

WALK IN THE SPIRIT

Strengthen Your Spirit, Not Your Flesh

Galatians 5:16–23

So I say, walk by the Spirit, and you will not gratify the
desires of the flesh. For the flesh desires what is contrary
to the Spirit, and the Spirit what is contrary to the flesh.
They are in conflict with each other, so that you are not to
do whatever you want. But if you are led by the Spirit, you
are not under the law. The acts of the flesh are obvious:
sexual immorality, impurity and debauchery; idolatry and
witchcraft; hatred, discord, jealousy, fits of rage, selfish
ambition, dissensions, factions and envy; drunkenness,
orgies, and the like. I warn you, as I did before, that those
who live like this will not inherit the kingdom of God.
But the fruit of the Spirit is love, joy, peace, forbearance,
kindness, goodness, faithfulness, gentleness, and
self-control. Against such things there is no law.

This section of the epistle points out that the believer has two
natures. We receive a new nature when we are born again
(2 Cor. 5:17), but God does not destroy our old carnal nature.
They reside side by side and are at war with one another. The
one that is the strongest always wins the battle.

How do we become strong physically? We become strong

by eating good nutritious food, exercising, and getting proper rest. To become stronger spiritually than we are carnally, believers take in as *food* the good Word of God on a regular basis, *exercise* obedience and the fruit of the Spirit, and *rest* in God. Whatever we feed and care for becomes strongest.

Paul says in Colossians that we are to "kill" the flesh (Col. 3:5 AMPC). As I pondered how to apply that thought practically, I realized that the best way to kill anything is simply not to feed it. The less we feed it, the weaker it becomes.

Each time we give in to the demands of the fleshly nature, we are feeding it and giving it strength to make more demands. But if we deny what it demands, then we are not feeding it and it becomes weaker and weaker.

Realizing that these two natures reside side by side illuminates the conflict we have experienced since we were born again. Sinful things we once practiced with no adverse feelings now bother us, and we feel guilty if we practice them. We cannot do them and remain peaceful in our hearts. We are convicted of doing wrong, and it makes us uncomfortable in our spirit. How quickly we mature spiritually depends on how quickly we submit or yield to the new nature and deny the old. We are spiritually sanctified at the new birth, but the process of working out our sanctification happens little by little as the Holy Spirit works with us and in us.

Once people receive Christ, they can no longer purposefully and continually practice sin because God's nature abides in them (1 John 3:9). They can sin, but they don't live in sin continually, and the longer they walk with God, the natural progression should be that they sin less and walk in the Spirit more and more.

This conflict will exist in us until the redemption of the body, which will be at the coming of the Lord Jesus Christ. At that time we will see an end to all temptation to sin. Until then the Holy Spirit helps us in our fight. He is our Helper!

Paul makes the point that recognizing the works of the flesh and the fruit of the Spirit is not difficult. He lists them both. The works of the flesh are:

- Sexual immorality
- Impurity
- Debauchery
- Idolatry
- Witchcraft
- Hatred
- Discord
- Jealousy
- Fits of rage
- Selfish ambition
- Dissensions
- Factions, or divisions
- Envy
- Drunkenness
- Orgies
- And the like

The fruit of the Spirit includes:

- Love
- Joy
- Peace
- Forbearance, or patience
- Kindness
- Goodness
- Faithfulness
- Gentleness
- Self-control

When I read these two lists, I feel stress simply reading the works of the flesh, and I feel peace while reading the fruit of the Spirit. It is not difficult for believers to know which way we should choose to live our lives.

I recommend that we focus on walking in the Spirit rather than trying *not* to walk in the flesh. What we focus on seems to become larger in our lives, and that ends up being what develops. Paul says, "Walk by the Spirit, and you will not gratify the desires of the flesh" (Gal. 5:16).

I spent many years trying not to walk in the flesh, and that actually seemed to cause me to walk in the flesh more. But when I realized that if I focused on walking by the Spirit there would be no room for the flesh, then and only then did I begin making real progress. I highly recommend starting your day spending some time with the Lord, talking to Him (prayer), studying His Word, and simply adoring and loving Him. You will find that these things help greatly to strengthen you for whatever you need to deal with throughout the day.

Personal Reflection

How does your life demonstrate the fruit of the Spirit?

_____

_____

_____

_____

_____

_____

Make a Full Surrender

We all receive the Holy Spirit and are sealed with the Spirit at the new birth, but not all are necessarily filled with the Holy Spirit at that time. I think we may say that it depends on whether or not the believer is ready to make a full surrender to God. Sometimes we want God in our lives to help us, but we have not surrendered our entire selves to Him. We want to make our plans and have God bless them. He wants something entirely different. He wants us to surrender completely to His will so He can prepare us to do whatever He might ask of us every day. Romans tells us what God desires from us and even makes the statement at the end that it is not an unreasonable request:

> I appeal to you therefore, brethren, *and* beg of you in view of [all] the mercies of God, to make a decisive dedication of your bodies [presenting all your members and faculties] as a living sacrifice, holy (devoted, consecrated) and well pleasing to God, which is your reasonable (rational, intelligent) service *and* spiritual worship.
>
> Romans 12:1 AMPC

I have pondered this verse many times and have been greatly blessed by it. We are to dedicate all of our faculties to God for His service. This means our thoughts, words, attitudes, actions, physical bodies, and emotions. That sounds to me like full surrender.

I was a Christian for many years before I became what I call a "serious Christian." I was the person who wanted God to help me, but I wasn't ready to surrender my entire life to Him. Through a great deal of misery and unhappiness, I finally did reach that point, and although I had the Holy Spirit prior to that time, once I was ready to fully surrender to God, I became filled with the Holy Spirit. Before that time, I had the Holy Spirit, but He didn't have all of me. I urge you to make a decision to surrender in all aspects of your life and walk by the Spirit.

Although full surrender is a one-time decision, you will have to renew your decision many times, perhaps daily. It is easy to commit to a diet Sunday evening after dinner, but the real test comes after a few days when you are hungry enough to eat everything you can get your hands on. When you make a decision to fully surrender to God's will, you will fail at times, but thankfully you can repent, receive forgiveness, let go of what is behind you, and begin again. God's mercy is new every day (Lam. 3:22–23).

Evidence That We Are Walking by the Spirit
Galatians 5:24–25

Those who belong to Christ Jesus have crucified the flesh with its passions and desires. Since we live by the Spirit, let us keep in step with the Spirit.

If we are walking by the Spirit there should be clear evidence of it, and Paul says the evidence is that we "have crucified the flesh with its passions and desires" (Gal. 5:24). I don't think the flesh can be entirely overcome in one swift blow, but we should be making steady progress in that direction as we grow in God. If I have been a Christian for twenty years and I am still behaving in the same immature, carnal way I did when I was born again, then I am not crucifying the flesh as God's Word instructs me to do. It's important to remember that this is not something we can do without God's help. His grace is what changes us, not our self-effort. However, we must desire to change, pray about it, study God's Word regarding the areas in which we need help, and endeavor, with the Holy Spirit's help, to pass each test that comes our way.

One of the many good things about walking with God is that if we fail a test, we always get to take it again. I recall praying for patience, and, wow, did I get opportunities to be patient! Many of them I would have rather not had, but patience is a fruit of the Spirit that only develops under trial. We cannot run away from difficulty, but we must remain steadfast while the difficulty does its work in our souls. I probably failed hundreds of times before I saw much improvement, and God and I are still working on it, but the good news is that I am making progress. Always notice your progress, not just your failures; otherwise, you will become discouraged and give up.

God loves the fact that you want to be all He wants you to be. He is proud of you! And He will never give up on you. If you keep taking one tiny step at a time, you will eventually cross the finish line.

Is there evidence in your life of spiritual growth? Can your family and friends see it? I'm sure they can. God has changed me so much in the forty-plus years since I surrendered to Him that my husband says he feels like he has been married to twenty different women in the fifty-three years we have been married. I just keep changing, and I know I still have a long way to go, but I am thankful that I am no longer where I once was. Progress is cause for celebration!

Personal Reflection

How are you making progress in your life, growing spiritually in ways that are evident in your attitudes and actions?

_____

_____

_____

_____

_____

_____

_____

Conceit and Jealousy

Galatians 5:26

Let us not become conceited, provoking and envying each other.

Paul ends this chapter with an exhortation for us not to "become conceited, provoking and envying each other" (Gal. 5:26). These are carnal traits, and Christians should avoid them. Sadly, we don't always avoid what we should avoid.

Jealousy and envy work through those who don't have their worth and identity firmly planted in Jesus Christ. When we know who we are in Jesus, we never need to be envious of anyone else. We should know that God has an individualized, special, perfect plan for each of us. It may not and probably won't be just like anyone else's, but it will be just right for us. Ask God for what you want and trust Him to give you what He knows is best.

Jealousy rots the bones (Prov. 14:30). That is a statement we should take seriously. We never get what someone else has by envying him or her. When John the Baptist's disciples tempted him to be envious of Jesus because the crowds were flocking to Him instead of to John (John 3:26), John quickly said, "A person can receive only what is given from heaven" (John 3:27). Knowing this truth kept John peaceful while things were changing in his life. He knew that the time had come for him to decrease and for Jesus to increase, and he was satisfied to fulfill the assignment God had given him. He was confident enough that he felt no need to compete with anyone. I am sure you will agree that that would be a wonderful freedom for anyone who possessed it.

Each of us should take responsibility for our own life and actions. Let's strive to be the best we can be without comparing ourselves with others. As we live by the Spirit, He will always lead us to the right place at the right time, and we will be able to enjoy the journey.

CHAPTER 14

◆—◇—◆

TRUE SPIRITUALITY

Becoming Truly "Spiritual"

Galatians 6:1

Brothers and sisters, if someone is caught in a sin, you who
live by the Spirit should restore that person gently. But
watch yourselves, or you also may be tempted.

Paul encourages us in our relationships with one another to
help restore anyone among us who is caught in sin. Rather
than being critical or judgmental toward them, we should
act in love and make every effort to help them. Let's say that
a Christian friend has been deeply hurt by someone and that
friend is angry and unwilling to forgive. If we notice this, we
should help restore that person, lest he or she sink deeper
and deeper into a problem that will cause spiritual harm.
When we try to help, we should do so in love and humility.

Paul is specific in saying who should attempt to restore
someone who has been trapped in sin. Those who do it should
be people who are spiritual, and they are to do it with a spirit
of gentleness. It is interesting to investigate how people define
spirituality. Some of the people who are involved in a great
deal of spiritual activity such as prayer meetings, Bible stud-
ies, good works, and regular church attendance and who give
generously would certainly seem to qualify as spiritual, or
as those "who live by the Spirit." However, quite often these

people are merely religious and self-righteous, and they do not display the fruit of the Holy Spirit that Paul writes about. I have known some very unkind Christians, and I imagine you have also.

We hear of the Desert Fathers, men who separated themselves from society, often going into the desert to live alone and seek God. One such man named Simeon the Stylite, or Simeon the Elder, lived from 390 to 459. He built a tower on the edge of the Syrian Desert and lived on top of it for many years. Surely, he was spiritual, we would think.

I have no right to judge whether Simeon was spiritual or not, but I will say that in my opinion behaving spiritually might be easier in a desert away from people than living spiritually in the midst of them and dealing with the stress of their imperfections and the trials of daily life. Spirituality usually doesn't grow in isolation but in community. I am sure I would have done a great deal of complaining had I tried living on top of a tower in the desert for six years. I would also have felt quite self-righteous about my sacrifice, and I would have secretly hoped that many people would come from the closest town to admire my sacrificial life. Those things alone could disqualify me from being "spiritual."

We live in a time when people are curious about spirituality, and there is no shortage of options for them to try. We have all kinds of New Age gurus, cults, covens, and spirit shops. We have so-called psychics who definitely consider themselves to be spiritual, and the list goes on. If Paul were alive today and saying that only someone "spiritual" is qualified to restore someone who has fallen into sin, he might change his wording. Perhaps he would say, "If anyone is caught in a sin, you who are born-again Christians, with godly behavior, living according to the Bible, and bearing the fruit of the Holy Spirit, should restore him." You see, the one who is qualified to restore another would have to be walking in the fruit of the Holy Spirit because gentleness is part of the fruit He produces in Christians.

A truly spiritual person would be one with some degree of spiritual maturity. He certainly would not need to be perfect, but neither could he be a baby Christian in his behavior. We often find that people who have recently been born again are so excited about their new life that they try to correct their families, friends, and co-workers who are not born again, and it rarely ends well. It usually causes those being corrected to avoid and even resent the new Christians.

The spiritual people Paul speaks about who are qualified to correct and restore others must be those who keep an eye on themselves so they are not also tempted. In other words, they don't think, *I certainly would never do that.* They realize that they are susceptible to temptation, and they live carefully, with caution regarding their behavior. They are people with humility, which is also something the Holy Spirit develops in us.

I have found that one of the best ways for me to approach the restoration of another person is to first share some of my own faults or some sin I have fallen into in the past. It also helps to share things I notice that the person is doing right.

Correction is one of the most difficult things for all of us to receive and be thankful for, and certainly it is much more difficult to receive if it does not come from someone who is kind and gentle. It is also difficult to receive if it is excessive. Being led by the Holy Spirit and proper timing are very important in the process of restoration. Very few people would endure having their faults brought to their attention all the time.

Gossip and Judgment

All too often, instead of true spiritual Christians ready to restore the sinner, we have an abundance of Christians ready to gossip and judge critically. Jesus gives us some very important instructions on how to treat someone caught in sin. When the woman was caught in adultery and the town was ready to stone her (John 8:1–11), Jesus said that the one among them who had no sin should be the one to throw the first stone (v. 7). They all walked away because not one of us is without sin, and we should remember this when dealing with others.

Jesus gives instructions through the apostle Matthew regarding how to deal with a fellow Christian who sins against us. He says we should go first to that person privately and tell him his fault. Hopefully he will listen and we will gain back our friend. If that doesn't work, then we should take two or three others with us so that two or three witnesses can confirm to that person what we are saying. If he or she still refuses to listen, we should tell it to the church, so they can deal with him or her properly (Matt. 18:15–17).

The Bible is filled with warnings about the dangers of gossip and judgment. We should remember that Jesus instructs us to treat others as we want to be treated (Matt. 7:12). Here are just a few Scriptures to consider:

A gossip betrays a confidence, but a trustworthy person keeps a secret.

Proverbs 11:13

A perverse person stirs up conflict, and a gossip separates close friends.

Proverbs 16:28

Do not judge, or you too will be judged. For in the same way you judge others, you will be judged, and with the measure you use, it will be measured to you. Why do you look at the speck of sawdust in your brother's eye and pay no attention to the plank in your own eye?

Matthew 7:1–3

Personal Reflection

How do you walk out Jesus' instruction to treat others
the way you want to be treated in your daily life?

_____

_____

_____

_____

_____

_____

_____

Caring for Those Who Are Hurting

Galatians 6:2–5

*Carry each other's burdens, and in this way you will fulfill
the law of Christ. If anyone thinks they are something
when they are not, they deceive themselves. Each one
should test their own actions. Then they can take pride
in themselves alone, without comparing themselves to
someone else, for each one should carry their own load.*

Paul tells us to "carry each other's burdens" and in doing
so, we will "fulfill the law of Christ" (Gal. 6:2), which is the
law of love. We should never think we are too good to put up
with something that is unpleasant for us and remember that
others sometimes have to put up with something unpleasant
about us, too. He says that if we think we are something or
someone of importance, when we are nothing except who we
are in Christ, we are deceived (Gal. 6:3). Satan loves to tell us
lies about our importance, and although we are very important to God, not one of us is too important to bear with the
failings of the weak or to carry another's burdens.

We should take a good, honest look at ourselves before
we boast and compare ourselves to our neighbors, thinking
we are better than they are. Telling those who are going to

restore a sinner that they should keep an eye on themselves also is Paul's way of saying to beware of spiritual pride. It is difficult to correct another's faults without feeling just a little self-righteous or superior, but that is something the spiritual person avoids.

Paul instructs us to "carry each other's burdens, and in this way you will fulfill the law of Christ" (Gal. 6:2). His letter to the Galatians is intended to remind them they are free from the law, but now he tells them to fulfill the law. He is talking about the moral law of love, which is the new commandment Jesus gives (John 13:34). Our salvation doesn't depend on fulfilling this law, but our level of spirituality is made clear by the fruit we display.

Christians have burdens. We are not promised lives without trials, heartache, and challenges. Multitudes of people struggle with worry, anxiety, fear, financial troubles, relationship problems, depression, loneliness, illness, and many other painful situations. We are to bear with them, which means to listen, to pray, to care, to make a phone call to check on them, or sometimes to simply sit with them. You may be in a season where life is good and you have no burdens, but there are others around you with burdens and they should not be forgotten.

I have people who work for me who struggle with illness, so I purposely ask how they are and let them know I am praying for them. There are others with broken hearts due to divorce or a child on drugs, and I ask how they are doing or if there is anything in particular I can pray about. This is what Christians should do for one another. We should care and reach out.

No one of us is too important to serve others. Paul actually says we are not to think of ourselves "more highly" than we ought to (Rom. 12:3). Instead, we are to refrain from selfish ambition, and "in humility value others above" ourselves (Phil. 2:3). Although we are not to think of ourselves in a downgrading or belittling way, we are to realize that in God's sight, our neighbors are just as valuable as we are.

Let's remember that although Jesus was "in very nature God," He didn't count His equality with God something to be grasped, but He "made himself nothing by taking the very nature of a servant" (Phil. 2:6–7).

Personal Reflection

Who can you reach out to and help to bear his or her burden?

_____

_____

_____

_____

_____

Don't Be a Dead Sea

Galatians 6:6

Nevertheless, the one who receives instruction in the word should share all good things with their instructor.

Reportedly, nothing can live in the Dead Sea because the water is stagnant. Fresh water flows into it, but none flows out. One of the greatest mistakes we can make is to be like the Dead Sea, being takers only and not givers. Some people become Christians because they want God to help them with their lives. They go to church to receive blessings. They expect others to help them, to pray for them, and to encourage them, but they do nothing for anyone else.

Paul says that those who are taught God's Word should "share all good things with their instructor" (Gal. 6:6). Always remember to thank the people who help you grow spiritually; write them a note of appreciation or give them a special gift. Pray for them and ask if you can do anything for them. We should always want our ministers to have a nice life with no financial burdens. They need to be able to give themselves to their ministries without the pressure of not being able to properly care for their families. The people who are always giving out to others have needs just as we do. And those who are spiritual realize that and make sure there is always something good flowing out of their lives as well as something good coming in.

Personal Reflection

How can you show your gratitude to people who have helped you grow spiritually?

_____

_____

_____

_____

_____

_____

CHAPTER 15

WE REAP WHAT WE SOW

It's All About the Seeds

Galatians 6:7–8

Do not be deceived: God cannot be mocked. A man reaps what he sows. Whoever sows to please their flesh, from the flesh will reap destruction; whoever sows to please the Spirit, from the Spirit will reap eternal life.

Paul now approaches another important spiritual truth, which is that God is not mocked and His principles cannot be set aside. He urges the Galatians—and us as well—not to be deceived into thinking we can behave badly and have good results. We reap what we sow.

I personally love this biblical truth because it lets me know that I have a measure of control regarding how my life turns out. Look down the road and ask yourself what you want your life to look like in the future, then be smart enough to realize that the seeds you sow today become the harvest you reap tomorrow.

We can see the principle of sowing and reaping easily when we think about gardening. We cannot sow onion seeds and reap tomatoes. We must sow the seed now that will produce the fruit or vegetable we desire to enjoy later.

God tells us in Genesis 8:22 that as long as the earth remains there will be seedtime and harvest. If you are not satisfied with your harvest, perhaps you should take time to look back at the seed you have been sowing. If people have no friends or they find that when they make new friends the friendships never last long, they would be wise to ask themselves how they treat their friends. Are they easy to get along with? Do they try to give others unwanted advice too often? Do they always sit and wait for the other person to pay the bill when they share a meal together? People who are good friends always have plenty of friends. People may not always remember everything you said, but they will remember how you made them feel.

If we sow mercy we will receive mercy (Matt. 5:7), and if we sow judgment we will receive judgment (Luke 6:37–38). We are frequently focused on our harvest, but perhaps we should be more focused on our seed.

Paul says that if we sow to the flesh, we will reap from the flesh. The Amplified Bible Classic Edition adds that if we sow to the flesh, we will reap from the flesh "decay *and* ruin *and* destruction" (Gal. 6:8). If we sow to the Spirit, we will reap life! We sow to the flesh by behaving in a fleshly, carnal manner, obeying the impulses of the flesh rather than following the guidance of the Holy Spirit. We do what we want to do rather than doing the will of God. Saul was a king who did not fully obey God, and he ultimately lost his kingdom as a result (1 Sam. 15:22–28). Our actions bring consequences, good or bad. A person may live like there is no tomorrow, but tomorrow always comes, and with it comes the harvest of the seeds we have sown in the past.

There are, of course, problems that come from the devil or merely as a result of living in the world, and we cannot avoid all of those, nor do we always sow some specific bad seed that causes them. But for anything over which we do have control, we should be careful to choose the more excellent thing or way and know that our efforts will be ultimately rewarded.

Personal Reflection

How can you sow good seeds in your life right now?

_____

_____

_____

_____

_____

_____

_____

Don't Grow Weary Doing What Is Right

Galatians 6:9–10

Let us not become weary in doing good, for at the proper time we will reap a harvest if we do not give up. Therefore, as we have opportunity, let us do good to all people, especially to those who belong to the family of believers.

It can be challenging when we are doing what is right and the right thing is not happening to us yet, but Paul urges us to not get weary of doing good or doing what is right. We should not do what is right just to get a reward, but we should do what is right because it is right. Sometimes that means we have to treat someone well for a long time before they begin to treat us well. Perhaps they will never treat us well, but our reward comes from God, not from other people.

I firmly believe that anyone who follows the principles of God consistently will end up with a good life. Those who come to God must "believe that he exists and that he rewards those who earnestly seek him" (Heb. 11:6). God's promises never fail. Their fulfillment may take longer than we would like, but if we don't get weary and we keep doing what is right, our reward will come.

Now Paul goes on to say something that I can say undoubtedly changed my life. Those who study God's Word usually have certain verses or passages that majorly impacted their lives, and Galatians 6:10 is one of those for me. In it, Paul says, "As we have opportunity, let us do good to all people, especially to those who belong to the family of believers." In the Amplified Bible Classic Edition, this verse reads, "Be mindful to be a blessing, especially to those of the household of faith." To be mindful means to have your mind full of something, or to purposefully think about it.

During a period of time when I was seeking to know what it meant in practical terms to love one another, this is one Scripture that gave me a simple instruction. And as I have followed it, my joy has increased. I have formed a habit of taking time to intentionally think of ways I can bless other people. I encourage you to ask God to show you how you can bless specific people in your life, and I believe He will. Learn to listen to people, because they usually tell you just in the course of conversation what they need, like, or want. If you are able, then try to make that happen for them. The less we have our minds on ourselves, the happier we become.

Recently a Christian couple we have known for many years asked if we would like to participate with a few others to pay the real estate taxes of a widow friend who was unable to pay them herself. The couple couldn't do it alone due to their own limited finances, but they went the extra mile and thought creatively about how the need might be met. They approached us as well as several other people, and within a few days the need was met. Imagine the widow's joy when she heard that she no longer had the pressure of paying the taxes hanging over her. If you hear of a valid need and cannot meet all of it, be bold enough to ask others to get involved. It is amazing what we can do together.

You might hear a friend or co-worker mention that their babysitter for Friday night canceled and they have been unable to find a replacement. Now they will have to miss something they were really looking forward to. Perhaps you know someone you could suggest, or you might even offer to keep the children yourself. You might overhear a single mom say that she hasn't been able to take her children out to eat in more than a year, and you could give her a gift certificate to a nice restaurant. I could go on forever making suggestions, but I'm sure you get the point. I urge you to not let opportunities to help others pass you by without at least giving some creative thought to what you might be able to do for them. It will be life changing!

Personal Reflection

How can you do good for someone who needs it?

_____

_____

_____

_____

_____

_____

_____

CHAPTER 16

FINAL WARNING

Revealing Wrong Motives

Galatians 6:11–13

See what large letters I use as I write to you with my own hand! Those who want to impress people by means of the flesh are trying to compel you to be circumcised. The only reason they do this is to avoid being persecuted for the cross of Christ. Not even those who are circumcised keep the law, yet they want you to be circumcised that they may boast about your circumcision in the flesh.

We can imagine that the moment described in Galatians 6:11–18 was charged with excitement. The Galatian church had gathered to hear a letter from none other than the apostle Paul himself. I am sure they were not expecting rebuke, because they may have been totally unaware of their wrong behavior. We should remember that they were deceived. They believed the lies of those who were trying to bring them under the law, so they were not aware of their error.

Paul often dictated his letters to a scribe or secretary, but he wants the Galatians to know that he is personally writing this letter to them. He wants it to have an impact, so he mentions that they will notice what large letters he is writing "with my own hand" (Gal. 6:11). Of course, they would know that he usually used a scribe because of his eye problem. We don't know what the specific problem was, but it might have been glaucoma or cataracts, or even a persistent infection, but it made it difficult for him to write his own letters. Hopefully, knowing that Paul wrote to them personally added to the importance of his message to them.

Paul reminds them that the people who were forcing them to be circumcised were only doing it to avoid persecution for the cross of Christ (Gal. 6:12). Most of us don't deal with the type of persecution they dealt with in the early church, so this may be difficult for us to understand. But being a Christian in those days was not popular and brought persecution in some way. Some of the persecution they experienced was quite severe, so they needed a lot of encouragement to remain steadfast. Paul urged them not to compromise in order to avoid persecution.

Paul also says that the ones who were circumcised didn't keep the law themselves (Gal. 6:13). In other words, they were hypocritical. They may have been circumcised, but the law demanded many other things they were not doing.

Boasting in the Cross

Galatians 6:14–16

*May I never boast except in the cross of our Lord Jesus
Christ, through which the world has been crucified
to me, and I to the world. Neither circumcision nor
uncircumcision means anything; what counts is the new
creation. Peace and mercy to all who follow this rule—to
the Israel of God.*

Paul says he has no reason to boast regarding his ministry or
any other good he might be doing, but that his only boast is
in the cross of Christ (Gal. 6:14). It is difficult to understand
the Greek word for *boast* in the English language. We might
think of it as to brag, but in Greek it meant much more. It
meant "to glory in," "to trust in," "to rejoice in," "to revel in,"
and "to live for." Whatever people boasted in had actually
become their obsession, and Paul's obsession was the cross
of Christ. To the Romans the cross was despicable and dis-
graceful. We have in our human history several centuries of
the cross being an object of hope and beauty, but in Paul's
day it was an object of horror and totally despised. Nonethe-
less, he boldly says it is his boast.

Sadly, we are seeing a trend concerning the cross of Christ
returning to being despised by many, and we frequently hear

of people trying to force others to remove crosses from buildings or printed materials because it offends some people. We must take a stand for what is right before we lose our rights.

Next, Paul makes a statement that is worth examining closely. He says, "The world has been crucified to me, and I to the world." What does he mean? "The world" refers to immoral and godless values, all the useless pursuits and hopeless pleasures of the world, meaning sinful humanity and those who are pursuing nothing but their own pleasures and self-will.

Paul says he is dead to all of that and it is dead to him. He has no relationship with those things any longer. *To be dead* means the cessation of being able to feel anything. Paul felt nothing, no pull or interest in anything connected to the world any longer. One might say he was ruined for anything but God. In other words, all those things that once were so important to him now held no importance at all. His only obsession was God and God's assignment to him to preach the gospel.

Paul reminds the Galatians again that being circumcised or not being circumcised doesn't count for anything (Gal. 6:15). The only thing with any spiritual value that really matters is that they are new creations in Christ. All those who live by this rule will experience peace and mercy.

Personal Reflection

Can you say, with Paul, that you are dead to the world? Explain why or why not.

_____

_____

_____

_____

_____

_____

_____

Trouble Me No More

Galatians 6:17–18

*From now on, let no one cause me trouble, for I bear
on my body the marks of Jesus. The grace of our
Lord Jesus Christ be with your spirit, brothers and
sisters. Amen.*

Paul states that no one is to trouble him anymore (Gal. 6:17).
He is apparently weary of their judgments and critical attitudes. He does not care what they think of him. He says he
bears on his body the marks of Jesus Christ. He has paid
the ultimate price for the One who paid the ultimate price
for him. He has been beaten many times while refusing to
stop preaching the gospel. He has been imprisoned, gone
hungry, been cold, and endured sleepless nights. All of that
took a toll on his physical body, and his scars could be seen.
He is declaring to those who have persecuted him that their
criticism and judgment no longer bother him and that they
should simply not waste their time trying to trouble him.

Paul may have had scars on his body, but in heaven he had
stars. His reputation on earth may not have been good from
a worldly perspective, but his reputation in heaven was great.

We must all decide where we want to be famous. Let us strive to be famous in heaven and not be concerned with our fame in this world. May God smile each day when we get up, and may the devil groan because he knows we will once again steal souls from him.

CLOSING COMMENTS

I pray you have been enriched by this biblical study on Galatians and that it has given you a deeper understanding of God's Word. You may want to review it at some future date, because you might find spiritual treasures you missed this time around. We are always growing spiritually, and I find that as I grow, my understanding of things I study grows also.

Anytime you feel you are being entrapped in religious legalism, return to this study on Galatians and remain steadfast in the liberty that Christ has given you.

Thank you for reading this book, and may God richly bless you every day of your life.

—Joyce

Do you have a real relationship with Jesus?

God loves you! He created you to be a special, unique, one-of-a-kind individual, and He has a specific purpose and plan for your life. And through a personal relationship with your Creator—God—you can discover a way of life that will truly satisfy your soul.

No matter who you are, what you've done, or where you are in your life right now, God's love and grace are greater than your sin—your mistakes. Jesus willingly gave His life so you can receive forgiveness from God and have new life in Him. He's just waiting for you to invite Him to be your Savior and Lord.

If you are ready to commit your life to Jesus and follow Him, all you have to do is ask Him to forgive your sins and give you a fresh start in the life you are meant to live. Begin by praying this prayer...

Lord Jesus, thank You for giving Your life for me and forgiving me of my sins so I can have a personal relationship with You. I am sincerely sorry for the mistakes I've made, and I know I need You to help me live right.

Your Word says in Romans 10:9, "If you declare with your mouth, 'Jesus is Lord,' and believe in your heart that God raised him from the dead, you will be saved" (NIV). I believe You are the Son of God and confess You as my Savior and Lord. Take me just as I am, and work in my heart, making me the person You want me to be. I want to live for You, Jesus, and I am so grateful that You are giving me a fresh start in my new life with You today.

I love You, Jesus!

It's so amazing to know that God loves us so much! He wants to have a deep, intimate relationship with us that grows every day as we spend time with Him in prayer and Bible study. And we want to encourage you in your new life in Christ.

Please visit **joycemeyer.org/knowJesus** to request Joyce's book *A New Way of Living*, which is our gift to you. We also have other free resources online to help you make progress in pursuing everything God has for you.

Congratulations on your fresh start in your life in Christ! We hope to hear from you soon.

ABOUT THE AUTHOR

Joyce Meyer is one of the world's leading practical Bible teachers. A *New York Times* bestselling author, Joyce's books have helped millions of people find hope and restoration through Jesus Christ. Joyce's programs, *Enjoying Everyday Life* and *Everyday Answers with Joyce Meyer*, air around the world on television, radio, and the Internet. Through Joyce Meyer Ministries, Joyce teaches internationally on a number of topics with a particular focus on how the Word of God applies to our everyday lives. Her candid communication style allows her to share openly and practically about her experiences so others can apply what she has learned to their lives.

Joyce has authored more than one hundred books, which have been translated into more than one hundred languages, and over 65 million of her books have been distributed worldwide. Bestsellers include *Power Thoughts*; *The Confident Woman*; *Look Great, Feel Great*; *Starting Your Day Right*; *Ending Your Day Right*; *Approval Addiction*; *How to Hear from God*; *Beauty for Ashes*; and *Battlefield of the Mind*.

Joyce's passion to help hurting people is foundational to

the vision of Hand of Hope, the missions arm of Joyce Meyer Ministries. Hand of Hope provides worldwide humanitarian outreaches such as feeding programs, medical care, orphanages, disaster response, human trafficking intervention and rehabilitation, and much more—always sharing the love and gospel of Christ.

JOYCE MEYER MINISTRIES

U.S. & FOREIGN OFFICE ADDRESSES

Joyce Meyer Ministries
P.O. Box 655
Fenton, MO 63026
USA
(636) 349-0303

Joyce Meyer Ministries—Canada
P.O. Box 7700
Vancouver, BC V6B 4E2
Canada
(800) 868-1002

Joyce Meyer Ministries—Australia
Locked Bag 77
Mansfield Delivery Centre
Queensland 4122
Australia
(07) 3349 1200

Joyce Meyer Ministries—England
P.O. Box 1549
Windsor SL4 1GT
United Kingdom
01753 831102

Joyce Meyer Ministries—South Africa
P.O. Box 5
Cape Town 8000
South Africa
(27) 21-701-1056

Other Books by Joyce Meyer

100 Ways to Simplify Your Life
21 Ways to Finding Peace and Happiness
Any Minute
Approval Addiction
The Approval Fix
The Battle Belongs to the Lord
Battlefield of the Mind*
Battlefield of the Mind for Kids
Battlefield of the Mind for Teens
Battlefield of the Mind Devotional
Be Anxious for Nothing*
Being the Person God Made You to Be
Beauty for Ashes
Change Your Words, Change Your Life
The Confident Mom
The Confident Woman
The Confident Woman Devotional
Do Yourself a Favor . . . Forgive
Eat the Cookie . . . Buy the Shoes
Eight Ways to Keep the Devil under Your Feet
Ending Your Day Right
Enjoying Where You Are on the Way to Where You Are Going
Ephesians: Biblical Commentary
The Everyday Life Bible
Filled with the Spirit
Good Health, Good Life
Healing the Soul of a Woman*
Healing the Soul of a Woman Devotional
Hearing from God Each Morning

*How to Hear from God**

How to Succeed at Being Yourself

I Dare You

*If Not for the Grace of God**

In Pursuit of Peace

James: Biblical Commentary

The Joy of Believing Prayer

Knowing God Intimately

A Leader in the Making

Life in the Word

Living beyond Your Feelings

Living Courageously

Look Great, Feel Great

Love Out Loud

The Love Revolution

Making Good Habits, Breaking Bad Habits

Making Marriage Work (previously published as *Help Me—I'm Married!*)

*Me and My Big Mouth!**

*The Mind Connection**

Never Give Up!

Never Lose Heart

New Day, New You

Overload

The Penny

Perfect Love (previously published as *God Is Not Mad at You*) *

The Power of Being Positive

The Power of Being Thankful

The Power of Determination

The Power of Forgiveness

The Power of Simple Prayer

Power Thoughts

Power Thoughts Devotional
Reduce Me to Love
The Secret Power of Speaking God's Word
The Secrets of Spiritual Power
The Secret to True Happiness
Seven Things That Steal Your Joy
Start Your New Life Today
Starting Your Day Right
Straight Talk
Teenagers Are People Too!
Trusting God Day by Day
The Word, the Name, the Blood
Woman to Woman
You Can Begin Again
Your Battles Belong to the Lord*

Joyce Meyer Spanish Titles

Belleza en Lugar de Cenizas (Beauty for Ashes)
Buena Salud, Buena Vida (Good Health, Good Life)
Cambia Tus Palabras, Cambia Tu Vida (Change Your Words, Change Your Life)
El Campo de Batalla de la Mente (Battlefield of the Mind)
Como Formar Buenos Habitos y Romper Malos Habitos (Making Good Habits, Breaking Bad Habits)
La Conexión de la Mente (The Mind Connection)
Dios No Está Enojado Contigo (God Is Not Mad at You)
La Dosis de Aprobación (The Approval Fix)
Efesios: Comentario Biblico (Ephesians: Biblical Commentary)
Empezando Tu Día Bien (Starting Your Day Right)
Hazte un Favor a Ti Mismo . . . Perdona (Do Yourself a Favor . . . Forgive)
Madre Segura de sí Misma (The Confident Mom)

Pensamientos de Poder (Power Thoughts)
Sanidad para el Alma de una Mujer (Healing the Soul of a Woman)
Santiago: Comentario Bíblico (James: Biblical Commentary)
Sobrecarga (Overload)*
Sus batallas son del Señor (Your Battles Belong to the Lord)
Termina Bien tu Día (Ending Your Day Right)
Usted Puede Comenzar de Nuevo (You Can Begin Again)
Viva Valientemente (Living Courageously)
* Study guide available for this title

Books by Dave Meyer

Life Lines